Roman
Mythology

LIBRARY OF THE WORLD'S
MYTHS AND LEGENDS

Roman Mythology

Stewart Perowne

PETER BEDRICK BOOKS
NEW YORK

Half-title page. Glaucus was a sea god, whom Virgil makes the father of the Sybil of Cumae. He designed the Argo and fought alongside the Argonauts.

Frontispiece. Apollo wearing a radiate crown drives his four-horsed chariot (or quadriga) through the sky. This detail from a mosaic pavement portrays Apollo as the sun-god following his daily flight across the heavens.

New revised edition first published in the United States in 1984 by Peter Bedrick Books, New York.

Second impression 1988

Roman Mythology first published 1969. New revised edition published 1983 by Newnes Books, a division of The Hamlyn Publishing Group Limited. Published by agreement with The Hamlyn Publishing Group Limited.

Library of Congress Cataloging in Publication Data
Perowne, Stewart, 1901–
    Roman mythology.

    (Library of the world's myths and legends)
    Bibliography: p.
    Includes index.
    1. Rome–Religion 2. Mythology, Roman. I. Title.
II. Series.
BL802.P46   1984   292′.3   84–6446
ISBN 0-911745-56-4 $32.95

Printed in Yugoslavia $26.35

Paulo Caruana Curran

Rerum Romanarum Indagatori Diligentissimo Melitae

A.S. MCMLXVIII

Contents

Introduction

The words Rome and religion are inseparable, because Rome is today and has been for close on two thousand years, the earthly fountain-head of a faith which is universal. This faith was brought to Rome from the east, from Jewish Palestine by way of the Greek orient, and implanted in Italy within a generation of the ministry of its founder. When in the year AD 61 the apostle Paul, himself a Greek-speaking Jew, arrived in Italy the Roman Christian community was well established. Many of its members were Jews, including relatives of his; but the majority, as we know from those named in the letter which Paul had written to them from Corinth four years earlier, were Gentile converts.

The arrival of Paul in Rome is generally taken to mark the beginning of an organised Roman Church, and thus of a new era. So in a sense it does; but the event raises two questions. The first is, from what were these Gentiles converted. The second is, why did they find in the unknown Christian faith, a Graeco-Semitic importation at that, something which the religion of their fathers did not supply.

It is to give an answer to these two questions that this study is designed. It will attempt to show first what were the origins of Roman religion, next how that religion developed as the Roman state developed, third how it failed to satisfy the individual Roman soul, fourth how two men of genius, one an emperor the other a poet, tried to turn the history of Rome into a religion and nearly succeeded, and finally how monotheism eventually prevailed, initially in its pagan form and then after a fierce

struggle, in its Christian form.

When we apply our mind's eye more closely to the scrutiny of the subject, we find that the focus is blurred by the golden mist of the *Graeco-Roman* concept. In the three centuries between the death of Alexander and the birth of Augustus the literature and arts – architecture most

notably – of Greece and Rome become so closely allied that it is easy to regard the resultant synthesis as an amalgam, even to see in early Roman nothing but late Greek. Nowadays the arts of Rome are recognised as existing in their own right. Roman religion must claim the same freedom. In fact the origins and early development of Roman religion were different from those of Greece and the destinies of the two people only coalesced at a mature stage. To understand therefore the actual nature of the religion of Rome today, a study of the origin and growth of earlier Roman religion may be not unprofitable.

The central area of the Forum seen from the west. The Palatine Hill is on the right.

Origins

The Romans started much later than the Greeks. In the Neolithic era, a people whom the Romans called Ligures, and we Ligurians, entered Italy. They came from North Africa, by way of Spain, and settled in the coastland round Genoa which we still know as Liguria. They were a tough, long-headed folk, and they survived into historical, indeed into imperial, times. At some date in the third millennium B.C. came other invaders, again from the north, as so many of Italy's later assailants were to come, bearing with them a wholly new element. That element was metal, and the metal was bronze. With bronze weapons went military ascendancy. To preserve it, the newcomers built orderly, defensible camps, trapezoidal in shape, and raised on stakes, a kind of lake-dwelling on land in fact, called a *terramara*. The word is derived from Italian country speech, and the plural is *terremare*. The *terramara* was the ancestor of the Roman camp. The terramarans were a good deal more advanced than the Ligurians, but they still could not write, and they lived in squalid villages. They were organised in exclusive clans. Their spoken language was probably the primitive forerunner of Latin.

In the eleventh century B.C. the Bronze-agers were supplanted by yet a third wave of northerners, armed this time with iron. They are known as Villanovans, from Villanova, a small town near Bologna where they were first identified in 1853. They were of a fairly high grade of civilisation, but it was not to be compared with the ancient river cultures of the Nile and Euphrates valleys. These northerners still could not write.

Upon these three strata, each one compounded of various elements and partially surviving its supplanter, was to be laid yet a fourth in the ninth century. This time the new arrivals were highly civilised. They came not from the barren north but from Asia Minor, and are known as Etruscans from the region of their principal settlement. Each year that passes brings us fresh evidence of the Etruscans' skill in painting, in metalwork, in sculpture, of their taste for good living and for maritime commerce. Of their religion we know little, because we cannot yet read their writing, but it seems to have been, in Rose's words, (*Primitive Culture in Italy*) 'elaborate, complex and gloomy. They laid great stress on divination in particular, and on the tendance of their dead, as is shown by the vast number of costly offerings which have from time to time been discovered'. These now adorn museums in Rome, Palestrina, Tarquinia and elsewhere.

Fifthly and finally in this catalogue of Rome's constituent elements we come to that which was in the end to prove the most potent of all, namely Greece. Not the mainland of Hellas, whose influence was not felt until later, but the Greek colonies in southern Italy, some of them hardly a hundred miles from Rome, and so numerous that the region was called *Magna Graecia*, Great Greece. To this day there are more Doric temples standing in Magna Graecia and Sicily than in Greece itself. The oldest of these colonies were founded in the eighth century, but the region's links with Greece go back to the thirteenth.

Only now do we come to the actual founding of Rome. At some time in the eighth century a primitive settlement appears on the Palatine, and with it Rome begins. But for the discussion of Roman religion we must keep in mind two facts. The first is that to identify the genuine Italic indigenous beliefs and practices we have to remove an overlay of Etruscan and Greek influence. 'If', to quote Rose again, 'we find for instance a rite described by Pausanias as alive in his day (i.e. in the second century A.D.) we may be pretty sure that we are dealing with a Greek practice of some sort; but if we find, in Virgil or Ovid (both poets of the Augustan age) a description of an Italian custom, we must examine his evidence very carefully before we can say he is telling us anything about Italic ways at all.'

What there was of Italic culture was a whole era, if not two, behind that of Greece. When the Etruscans came to Italy; bringing with them the art of writing which they seem to have learned from the Greeks, the Homeric poems were already a century old; and the Homeric poems, be it remembered, recall and record many deeds, many cities and many artefacts of far older times. The civilisation of Crete had come to an end more than half a millennium before, to be followed by that of Mycenae. The citadels of Mycenae and Tiryns, the tombs and palaces at Pylos, the jewellery, the gold vessels and ornaments and arms in the National Mu-

seums at Athens and Herakleion in Crete still astound the modern beholder. All of this august glory was the birthright, the patrimony of the classical Greek culture which was now coming to birth, at a time when the Romans, the future masters of Greece and the world were still, technically, savages. Savagery had therefore to survive for only a comparatively short time to leave an abiding mark on the religion of the Roman republic and empire, and that is precisely what it did.

Above. Etruscan panel from funerary urn, probably from Volterra, 150-100 B.C.. It depicts a couple on their way to the underworld accompanied by attendants. British Museum, London.

Right. Pan. This very ancient god comes from Arcadia. Here he is playing on the syrinx, or pan-pipes, as Papageno does in Mozart's *Magic Flute*, and shepherds in Arcadia still do. Etruscan bronze *c*. 430 BC. British Museum, London.

Opposite. Relief on the back of an altar depicting Romulus and Remus. At the base the twins are being suckled by the famous wolf. The Romans were fond of this kind of visual 'strip' narrative, as vividly used on the Columns of Trajan and Marcus Aurelius still standing in Rome. Musei Vaticani.

Gods

Romulus is traditionally held to have founded Rome in the year 735 B.C. It was strategic necessity rather than amenity that dictated its position. Romulus and his clan were Latins, who lived in Latium, the district south and west of the Tiber valley. The site of Rome was determined by the necessity of having a bulwark or strong-point which would be easily defensible against the pressure of the Etruscans from the north. Only where the hills of Rome, in particular the Palatine and the Capitol, front the river bank, some twenty miles from the mouth of the Tiber, does such a site exist. Moreover it is here that the Tiber is first fordable, thus providing a vital north-south link. So it was on those two hills nearest the river that the first settlement or settlements arose. Other hills such as the Quirinal were soon populated, and the space outside the hamlets, at that time a marsh, became the common meeting-place and market. The Latin for outside is *foras*, and so the space became known as the Forum.

Early Romans and their Beliefs

These first Romans were primitive folk, which meant that each clan must have had more or less friendly relations with some other in order to find itself wives; for the clan was a family, and to marry within it would be taboo, incest in fact. This search for wives is the subject of one of Rome's earliest and best-known myths, the 'Rape of the Sabines', where the ladies were obtained by fraud and force, peaceful relations being later restored. The story is charming; but the underlying fact is a valuable pointer to the stage of social evolution beyond which the first Romans

had not yet progressed.

What were their religious beliefs? From the burials of the peoples described in the last chapter – and be it remembered that we have nothing else to go by – whether they were inhumed or cremated, it is clear that they believed in the survival of the dead, either corporally in another world or as spirits to be placated in this one. These beliefs were certainly held by Rome's founders; but what actual gods did they worship?

Roman gods were completely different from those of Greece. The Greeks were polytheists. Their gods were individuals, beings, just like human beings; in fact some gods like Asklepios, god of healing, started as mortals. Others, such as Heracles, were half mortal and half divine. But when we think of them we think of fully developed personalities. About Apollo, for instance, whole books have been written, so many-splendoured, so beautiful were his character and attributes. The visitor to Delos or Delphi can with no great difficulty and with much profit meditate on the gifts of this god of light, the lord of all brightness in thought and form; just as the pilgrim to Assisi or Avila may be fortified by the recollection of Saint Francis or Saint Teresa. With Roman gods no such exercise is possible. Vulcan is the god of fire. Fire is destructive and so Vulcan was usually worshipped outside the city. His feast was on the twenty-third of August, and the celebrant threw into the flames little fish, which were held to represent human lives for the preservation of which they were offered. And that is all we know about Vulcan. He has no mythology at all: he is just a tough, prac-

Below left. Hercules felling a centaur. The centaurs were wild creatures, half horse half human, who were always causing trouble – except Chiron, who was good, and brought up Achilles, Jason and Asklepios. From a group in Florence by Giovanni Bologna. (1524–1608).

Below. Another statue of Hercules in Florence, by Baccio Bandinelli (1488–1560). He is seen subduing Cacus, son of Vulcan, who lived in a cave on the Aventine, into which he had dragged Hercules' cattle, backwards, to lay a false trail.

tical Roman craftsman. Later, as in the case of so many Roman deities, Vulcan was identified with a Hellenic counterpart, in his case the Greek artificer-god Hephaistos, and we find him married to Venus and making a shield for Aeneas.

Compared with the Greek pantheon, Roman gods of comparable stature, what have conveniently been called 'high' gods, were few in number. There was a triad of high gods, namely Jupiter (properly but pedantically spelt Juppiter), Mars and Quirinus; and Jupiter himself was the central figure of another triad, being flanked by the goddesses Juno and Minerva. This latter triad was the principal focus of Roman veneration. The Roman Capitol was its dwelling-place. In the most high and palmy state of Rome, when countless cities owned her sway, it was the first care of a city's architect to raise a capitol analogous to that of Rome, and on it to instal the three deities, with Jupiter enthroned in the midst.

Jupiter and his Consorts

By the time Rome had become an imperial power, Jupiter had become assimilated to the Greek Zeus, and had taken on much of his glory; but his origins were humble enough. Like the first Romans he came from Latium, and his sanctuary was on what is now Monte Cavo, to the east of lake Albano and not far from the summer residence of the Pope. No trace of the shrine now remains, its place having been taken by a convent built by Cardinal York, the last of the Stuarts, now an inn, and more recently also by a television transmitter. Jupiter was the supreme god of the confederation of the forty-seven Latin cities, and they met here for their celebrations every spring and autumn.

Above left. Detail of the famous Belvedere Apollo, a marble copy of a Greek original, probably bronze, of the fourth century B.C., generally attributed to Leocares. The young god is marking the effect of the arrow he has just released from his bow. Found at Grottaferrata at the end of the fifteenth century. Musei Vaticani.

Above right. Jupiter was the god of light and sky who in time became the great protector of city and state. He symbolised the virtues of justice, good faith and honour. In addition, Jupiter was a warrior-god whose aid was invoked before any military undertaking and a portion of the spoils of war was always offered to him. The annual games. The *ludi romani*, were celebrated in his honour. Fresco of Jupiter enthroned, from the house of the Vetii in Pompeii.

Left. Vulcan had his own *flamen*, and his festival, the *Volcanalia*, was celebrated on the twenty-third day of August. Vulcan had no legends of his own, but was assimilated to Hephaistos, the Greek god of fire. From a bust in the Musei Vaticani.

Opposite above. Tarpeia, on the rock, part of the Capitol, named after her, about to be smothered by the ungrateful Sabines to whom she had thought to betray the Citadel. In later days certain types of malefactors were precipitated from the Tarpeian Rock. From a relief in the Basilica Aemilia in the Forum.

Opposite below Juno Lucina, goddess of childbirth. In this Roman bronze mask she looks frightening rather than comforting; but Roman mythology was based largely on terror rather than love. Magyar Nemzeti Muzeum, Budapest.

On the Capitol Jupiter was worshipped in several guises, of which Jupiter Feretrius 'the smiter,' was the oldest. It was to him, men said, that Romulus had dedicated the spoils he had taken when he killed the Sabine king Acron. As the god of lightning he was known as Jupiter Elicius, from the verb *elicere*, to attract. It was he who attracted the lightning from heaven, and above all, allowed the sorcerer to make it come down. Later on Jupiter was worshipped as Optimus Maximus, the Best and Greatest, a designation which was to be carried over into Christianity and appears on many a monumental inscription, often abbreviated to D.O.M., Deo Optimo Maximo. This cult was imported from the Quirinal, at the same time as Juno and Minerva were similarly translated. There was another temple of Jupiter, also ascribed to Romulus, down in the Forum, where the arch of Titus now stands. It was dedicated to Jupiter Stator, or 'stayer', because it was here that in answer to Romulus' prayer he had stayed the flight of the Romans before the Sabines and had given them the victory.

Before we trace the later development of Jupiter, because as time went by, and especially after his synthesis with Zeus, he became grander and grander, it may be well to introduce his two consorts, Juno and Minerva; and secondly to discover, if we can, just what the first Jupiter was. Here we must make a cardinal point in regard to Roman religion: it was not static, it was not dogmatic, it was not even doctrinal. In this it was wholly unlike the monotheistic religions of our day, Judaism, Christianity and Islam. There was no question of a revelation, of a Law, of a Faith once for all delivered. Belief and practice varied from age to age, and as the years unfolded religion bcame more and more eclectic.

Juno was originally the goddess of the moon, a most important deity in primitive societies, who rely on the moon for the calendar by which they regulate their agricultural cycle. She was, as noted above, originally worshipped on the Quirinal; but she had

other shrines as well, of which the most interesting for us is that of Juno Moneta, 'she who warns', a title bestowed upon her because it was her sacred geese who had given the warning when the Gauls were assaulting Rome in 390 B.C., and so saved the Capitol. It was also in this temple, that, as a thank-offering to Juno for her help in overcoming the Epirot invader Pyrrhus in 275 B.C., the coins of Rome were struck, and it is from the Latin *moneta* that we get our English words 'mint and 'money'. Juno was the protectress of women in general, and specially in childbirth. She was later assimilated to Hera, who was not nearly such a nice character, but being the wife of Zeus, had to be admitted with him.

Minerva is said to have been introduced into Rome by Numa, the second king of Rome whose traditional dates are 715-673 B.C. She seems to have come from Etruria. She was later assimilated to Athene and as such presided over all intellectual activity, schools in particular. On the Esquiline hill there was a chapel of Minerva Medica, and *ex-votos* recovered from a ruin in the vicinity show that the cult was still in vogue during the empire.

Now we must go back to Jupiter. What did he look like to his earliest worshippers? It is rather a shock to find that he was neither godlike nor human; he was just an old stone, Jupiter Lapis. In the temple of Jupiter Feretrius already mentioned were preserved some ancient flint-stones. To bind himself by the strongest possible oath – and the practice was still observed in the days of Cicero – a man would say: 'If I knowingly deceive, may Jupiter, without harm to the city or the citadel, cast me forth as I cast this stone', hurling it as far as he could. Even more striking was the ceremony for ratifying a treaty, because here the whole state *was* involved. One of the Fetiales, the ancient college of twenty priests who advised on international affairs, killed a pig with a flint-stone from the same shrine and said: 'If the Roman people shall be the first to transgress this treaty by common consent, and of malice aforethought, then Jupiter do you on that day strike the Roman people even as on this day I smite this pig, and smite it harder, because you are stronger and more mighty'. Clearly the stone (or stones, for so holy an object must have been supplied with reserves) was older than Jupiter. It goes back to neolithic days, perhaps even before them, the stones being no doubt old flint knives or axe-heads. When the metal-users arrived they associated these venerable and rather terrifying flints with the greatest deity they knew, the god of light, Jupiter, who among other functions was the punisher of perjurors.

Mars and Quirinus

When we turn to the second of the 'high' triad, Mars, we find much the same state of affairs. The origins of Mars are obscure because here again we know him mostly as assimilated to Ares, the Greek god of war. Mars was the Roman god of war but he also has agrarian attributes. His festivals fell mostly within the month which still bears his name. As the 'off-season' for both war and agriculture was the same in antiquity, namely from autumn to spring, his dual role is perfectly logical. Now down in the Forum there stood a house called the Regia, originally, as its name shows, the dwelling of the kings of Rome. In it were preserved spears called the spears of Mars, of which one at least was actually known as Mars.

Similarly with the last of the 'high' triad, Quirinus. He was a war-god, of Sabine origin, and dwelt on the Quirinal, which was a Sabine settlement. It is today the official seat of the Italian government. Quirinus has almost no history or mythology, apart from his identification with the deified Romulus; but certain weapons

Right. Numa, who ruled Rome from 762 to 716 B.C. He was a Sabine. He is by tradition the religious king *par excellence*, and is credited with the founding of many of Rome's cults, including that of the deified Romulus under the name of Quirinus. Bust from the Museo di Villa Albani, Rome.

Left. On the left, Mars and Rea Silvia, daughter (or descendant) of Aeneas, and mother of Romulus and Remus. On the right, Diana and Endymion. From a relief in the Musei Vaticani.

Opposite left. The famous Ludovisi Mars, or Ares. The god is shown gazing into the distance with an almost dreamy expression. The *amorino* at his feet shows that he is thinking of Venus, or Aphrodite. The naturalism of the treatment suggests Lysippus (fourth century B.C.) as the original artist. Museo Nazionale Romano, Rome.

Opposite right. A statue from the Musei Vaticani showing Mars in his role of god of war.

known as the arms of Quirinus were ritually anointed by a priest of the god of gates, Portunus. We do not know why, but the fact that they were anointed shows that they were regarded as being in some way alive, and as possessing the vital quality which the Romans called *numen*. The word means literally 'nod', the idea being that if you were a god, you need not lift a finger: all you had to do was to nod, and your will would be done.

The Other Gods

So much for the 'high' gods of Rome and their consorts: in every case we find the relics of savagery. The first Romans really did 'bow down to wood and stone'. When we look a little deeper into their heaven, we are amazed at the proliferation of gods, and at the insubstantiality of them. They are either lifeless things, or phantoms, little more than names. There was an old gate down in the Forum which was never used for any practical purpose, because it was on the line of no wall. It was called *Janus*. Janus was the god of gates, and gave his name to the first month of the year. But not only was he the god of the gate, he was the gate itself: he and those stones were one, and from that gate he could preside over all the gates, all the doors of the buildings in Rome.

Another such stone was Terminus, the boundary god. Terminus marked the limit of a man's property, and so made for harmony between neighbours, a vital function in a farming community. The stone was solemnly oiled and garlanded, and then lowered into a hole which had already been hallowed with the blood of a victim and with wine and other offerings. Every year on 23 February (which in the primitive calendar was reckoned as the last or terminal day of the year) the neighbours whose lands Terminus divided met and sacrificed a pig or lamb, brought other offerings, and garlanded the terminus and sprinkled it with the blood of the sacrifice. Thus the *numen* was revived for another year, to stand as safeguard of property from any aggressor.

Above. Statue of Jupiter from the Villa Albani showing the god with one of his thunderbolts in his left hand. Museo di Villa Albani, Rome.

Right. Juno the majestic queen of heaven and wife of Jupiter. Museo Archeologico Nazionale, Naples.

Opposite. Minerva was the goddess of the arts and handicrafts. In one hand she is holding an owl, which symbolized wisdom. Musée du Louvre, Paris.

Below. Janus, one of the oldest of Roman gods. It was he who frustrated Tarpeia's plan to betray the day to the Sabines; for which reason in times of war his temple was always to be left open, so that he could go to the instant aid of the Romans. It was shut only when Rome was at peace.

When we turn to the lesser gods, we meet an almost innumerable company. There were gods and goddesses for every conceivable situation, action and predicament. Sometimes indeed men did not know whether the *numen* they addressed was male or female. The dedication *si deus si dea*, 'be you god or goddess' is by no means rare, and an altar with this legend stands on the Palatine to this day. These gods were invoked right up to the end of paganism. Christian writers, as late as the fifth century, were constrained to inveigh against them, which Saint Augustine does with much wit. Talking of the *numen* of Juno Moneta, mentioned above, he says that when the Gauls attacked 'the geese stayed awake while the gods slept'. There was a temple of Concord: would not Discord be a more popular dedication? And, in a state which had waxed great on war, why not a temple to External Aggression? To guard the doorway, Augustine notes, three gods are needed, one for the threshold, one for the door itself, and a third for the hinge, whereas a single porter, being *human*, does the job. Three *numina* in the same way, were needed to uproot, take away and burn a tree which had sown itself unwanted on a temple roof. These *numina* (which remind us of the restrictive practices of some modern trades unions) seem to be little more than the names they bear.

22

Above. Cloaca Maxima, the main drain of ancient Rome, said to have been opened by Tarquinius Priscus, sixth century B.C., but only the embankment might go back to that epoch. The present vault is not earlier than the second century B.C. (see picture and caption on page 21).

Opposite. A triton on an Etruscan amphora. Tritons were a lower race of sea-gods. Museo Nazionale di Villa Giulia, Rome.

Many of these *numina* were beneficent, Spiniensis, for instance, who helped you to clear your field of thorns, or Stercutius who saw to the manuring of it, or Cloacina who looked after the sewers. But others were not. Febris brought fever, malaria, and was attended by Tertiana and Quartiana (a dedication to Tertiana has been found at Risinghám in northern England). She must be placated. So, too, must the dread Robigus, the god of rust or mildew. A special day was set apart for him, 25 April, when a dog, which would presumably have been a red, rust-col-oured dog, was sacrificed to him.

For if men needed gods at every turn, the gods needed men to keep them happy. There was a special sacrificial formula in use at Rome, *macte esto*, which means 'may you be increased or made great', 'magnified' in fact in the religious sense. Roman religion at this stage was akin to Roman law: it was a bargain. 'I give that you may give', they said to the gods, or in other words, 'My will be done on earth.' The measures by which they sought to obtain this happy outcome must now be briefly examined.

Worship

Readers of the Bible are familiar with the evolution of Yahweh, the primitive tribal god, into the sublime, universal Spirit of the Prophets, the God of Jew and Christian alike, and one of the loftiest religious ideas ever conceived by man. Roman religion shows no such parallel. The official religion of Rome continued from first to last to embody and to employ survivals from the age of savagery. This is one reason why, as already noted, the religion of the individual Roman became more and more eclectic.

Many of the rites associated with Roman *numina* took place out of doors, just as today religious processions are among the main manifestations of the Catholic faith in Italy. Such processions go back to a very remote antiquity indeed, to an era before temples were in use; because it is only when people moved from the open field or the tent into a more permanent dwelling that they thought that the god, too, should have his own house, instead of being left to wander about or at best being housed in a tabernacle. One such early survival is the rite known as lustration. The verb *lustrare* means to purify, but it also means to move in a solemn procession, and so to purify by procession. 'Beating the Bounds' survives in England as a picturesque piece of folklore, but its original purpose was the same as that of lustration, namely to protect by encircling. No-one really believes that the choirboys and wands of Rogationtide in England are having any practical effect on the crops. In Rome they did.

Cato

Of all the hard, unbending Roman republicans the elder Cato is often regarded as the archetype. He is also the father of Latin prose, the earliest Latin writer of whom we have any coherent work. His views therefore on men and gods are of special interest. He owned large plantations which were worked by slaves. He was an absentee landlord, being busy in Rome, where in season and out of season he demanded that Carthage be destroyed. (He died in 149 B.C.: Carthage was razed to the ground three years later.) He wrote a manual of husbandry, or how to run a farm with the maximum profit; Cato's standards of humanity may be inferred from the following passage which occurs near the beginning of the handbook: 'Sell worn-out oxen, blemished cattle, blemished sheep, wool, old tools, and old slaves, sickly slaves and whatever else is superfluous'.

For Cato, religion was purely contractual. The housekeeper, he directs, is to stay indoors and not to go gadding about visiting and gossiping with the neighbours; and she certainly must not attend divine worship: the head of the family will take care of that for one and all. But when it comes to Cato's own property, then religion is to be used, simply because it may prove useful: 'If the steading is struck by lightning, an expiatory prayer must be said'. A sick ox is to be cured by administering the crushed head of a leak and 'both the ox and the one who administers must stand,

The Temple of Vesta in the Forum. This charmingly feminine building was round because it imitated the shape of the first primitive huts of the Latins. The Regia is partly visible on the left of the building. The Vestals' house was immediately to the right of it.

and both must be fasting'. So we are quite prepared for his instructions in regard to lustration, the beating of the bound or *ambarvalia* ('round the fields') as it was called.

First, his factor must prepare the *suovetaurilia*, that is, three victims, a swine, a ram and a bull – *sus, ovis, taurus*. Then: 'The following is the formula for preparing land: bidding the suovetaurilia to be led around, use the words "That with the good help of the gods success may crown our work, I bid you, Manius (an overseer), to take care to purify my farm, my land, my ground with this suovetaurilia, in whatever part you think it best for them to be driven or carried around". Make a prayer with wine to Janus and Jupiter, and say, "Father Mars, I pray and beseech you to be gracious and merciful to me, my house, and my household; to which intent I have bidden this suovetaurilia to be led about my land, my ground, my farm, that you keep away, ward off and remove sickness, seen and unseen, barrenness and destruction, ruin and unseasonable influence; and that you allow my harvests, my grain, my vineyards and my plantations to flourish and to come to good issue, preserve in health my shepherds and my flocks, and give good health and strength to me, my house and my household. To this intent, to the intent of purifying my farm, my land, my ground and of making an expiation, as I have said, be magnified (*macte esto*) by the offering of these suckling victims. Father Mars, to the same intent be magnified by these suckling victims".' Cakes are to be offered; and if any of the victims fails to yield favourable omens another must be substituted for it.

Now all this must seem to us to be very far from what we know as religion, and so it is: it is simply contractual magic. The suovetaurilia remained in vogue right down to the days of the empire; and there is a famous representation of it, dating from the time of Trajan and originally probably part of the Rostra, in the Curia or senate-house in the Forum. Indeed, the ambarvalia has in essence lasted very much longer, right down to our own days. In the town of Loreto Aprutino in the Abruzzi, on Whit Monday a fine white ox, the offering of one of the citizens, is led through the town to the accompaniment of fireworks and music, with a small boy astride it. Up to and including 1949, the ox entered the church, where it had been trained to kneel before the image of the local patron, a rather faint-haloed saint called San Zopito. But, to quote the book of the present mayor, Signor Michele Vellante, 'From Whit Monday, 1949, notwithstanding the lively protests of the villagers, by the will of the *abate* Mgr Remo di Carlantonio, the ox of San Zopito has entered the church no more'. (The *abate* was a courageous man: the last one who tried to banish the ox, was taken ill and died in no time. That was in 1876.) The festival lasts three days, during which the ox visits the houses and collects money, distributing in return its own offering to Stercutius, from the liberality of which the harvest prospects are forecast. Finally the ox and his conductors visit the house of a local nobleman where they are made welcome and fêted.

Iguvium Tablets
We must now refer to what have been described by the *Oxford Classical*

Suovetaurilia, a very ancient form of Roman sacrifice, which lasted into imperial times. In this relief *left*, an emperor is seen offering it. The victims were a pig, a sheep and a bull, whence the name. 'Il Bue di San Zopito', a modern equivalent of the ancient Roman suovetaurilia which, as described in the text, continues to this day. Musée du Louvre, Paris. The picture (*opposite left*) kindly supplied by the Mayor of Loreto, shows a recent celebration of the ceremony. Note the bagpiper.

Dictionary as 'surpassing all other documents for the study of Italic religion', namely the famous Iguvine Tablets. In the year 1440, at Gubbio, the ancient Iguvium in Umbria, nine bronze tablets came to light, engraved on both sides partly in the Latin alphabet and partly in the Umbrian, the language itself being Umbrian. Two of the tablets were taken to Venice and lost, but seven still survive in Gubbio. The oldest was written in 400 B.C., the latest in 90 B.C. The text contains the proceedings and liturgy of a brotherhood of priests, namely the directions for a lustration of Iguvium, for an assembly of the *populus* of Iguvium, the concluding sacrifice of the lustrum on behalf of the Brotherhood, the optional sacrifice of a dog to an infernal deity called *hontus*, and directions for a sacrifice to Jupiter and to a medley of gods of the upper and lower worlds with outlandish names.

In regard to the actual ritual, Rose points out that there are three points of importance for the study of the links between religion and magic. First, no foreigners may attend the rite. No Tadinate people, no Tuscan,

no Narcan folk, nor any Iapudic, shall be there. This ban is imposed not to prevent strangers from learning what is going on, but because a stranger would have a bad effect on the family magic. Shakespeare employs the same device in *The Phoenix and the Turtle* to 'keep the obsequies so strict'.

Secondly, no one, not even a citizen, must hear the actual words of the liturgy. This again is common magic practice. It was the general custom in antiquity, as it is today, that common prayer should be offered audibly; but certain supplications were too 'strong', too charged with power, to be spoken aloud. Today, certain parts of the Catholic mass may be recited either silently or in so low a voice that the congregation cannot hear them.

Thirdly, the ritual must be absolutely word perfect. If it is interrupted or if the smallest mistake is made, then all must be done again. This was common Roman practice; but it could be not only vexatious but expensive as well, if a whole new set of victims had to be provided, as happened once at the *feriae Latinae*, or

festival of the Latin League mentioned in the last chapter. The celebrant of the small town of Lanuvium got the designation of the Roman people wrong. Lanuvium had to pay, but it was Rome that felt the wrath of the gods, because one of the consuls had a stroke on his way back from the maimed rites and died soon after. The Iguvians were more canny: they took prophylactic action. Part of their ceremony consisted in sacrificing three fatted oxen to Jupiter *Grabovius*, or 'of the oak-tree'. In the prayer before the sacrifice the god is thus addressed: 'Jupiter Grabovius, if in your sacrifice any mistake has been made, anything done wrong, or if anything has been lost or any fraud or offence committed, if there has been a mistake whether noticed or not, then Jupiter Grabovius if it be right to do so, let it be atoned for by the sin-offering of this fattened ox'.

A corollary to the insistence on the sanctity of ritual words spoken either aloud or inaudibly was that no other sound should intrude, no words of ill-omen be heard. It was for that reason, and to drown any discordant note, that grand ceremonials such as triumphs were accompanied with music and cymbals. Here again the petards and bagpipes of Loreto – or of Malta and Gozo – are only perpetuating a very ancient custom.

In this field of the religio-magic two other typically Roman manifestations may be noted. The first concerns spell-casting, the use of *carmina*. The Latin word *carmen* gives us our word 'charm'. Originally it meant a song, and as such it was commonly used. Horace describes his Odes as *carmina*. But the word had a more sinister meaning. The earliest known Roman code of law, the Twelve Ta-

bles of the mid-fifth century B.C. forbade the singing of *carmina* against anyone. That did not mean it was unlawful to sing rude songs about people – on the contrary, that practice was encouraged in the case of great folk such as triumphing generals in order to turn aside the envy of vindictive spirits. What was made illegal was the casting of spells. Virgil used the word in the same sense. It was by means of *carmina* that Circe changed the companions of Ulysses into swine; Dido knew a priestess who used *carmina* to cure love-pains. Charms could also be used, Virgil

Opposite left. Vestal, from a statue found in the House of the Vestals. The garb and aspect of the figure recall those of a nun, of which the Vestals were in many ways the Roman analogue. Museo Nazionale Romano, Rome.

Opposite right. Vestal. A bronze from near Capua. The figure is holding a horn symbolising the *penus* or store, which was renewed at the annual festival of Vesta in June. Musée du Louvre, Paris.

Below. A relief showing five of the six Vestals looking attentively at the goddess (not shown here). Note again the container and the statuettes of bull and sheep indicative of earth's gifts. Museo Nazionale, Palermo.

tells us, to increase the abundance of a man's crop at the expense of his neighbour; and this, too, was proscribed by the Twelve Tables.

Vesta and her Fire

Finally we come to a part of the Roman cult which was to remain of great importance throughout the history of Rome, namely, the worship of Vesta and the custody of her undying fire by the Vestal Virgins. Why is it that they play so prominent a part in Roman life? They were treated with the greatest respect, they were allotted special seats in the theatre, their house was used as the repository for wills. If their chastity was violated, they were to die a horrible death by being buried alive – an ordeal, really, because Vesta could always intervene to save the innocent. The reason for their importance seems to be the following. As will already have appeared, Roman primitive religion was a family affair, with the head of the family in charge; and its manifestations were all connected with the welfare of family and farm. It was concerned solely with personal and material benefits, without any but the most rudimentary moral or ethical overtones. Now the seat of the family is the home, and the focus of the home is the hearth. (The Latin word *focus* means hearth.) The tending of the hearth had always been relegated to younger unmarried daughters, of whom Cinderella is the best known example, because paterfamilias was busy out of doors, and materfamilias in the kitchen or at the loom. So the *numen* of the hearth was naturally regarded as feminine. Vesta was extremely venerable, and belonged to the 'inner circle' of the twelve gods of whom we shall be speaking later. Near the hearth there would be a cupboard, called a *penus*, in which provisions were stored. The spirits attendant on it were called Penates, the Lares being phantoms responsible for the house as a whole. The Lares were also in charge of cross-roads; and there was a curious legend that one of them, assuming the substance of a phallus amid the coals of the hearth, had intercourse with a slave

of Queen Tanaquil, wife of king Tarquin, who was guarding the fire and thus became the father of king Servius Tullius. The core of the legend is an acknowledgement of the divine potency of fire.

The king's hearth (as the foregoing story illustrates) would naturally be rather more important than anyone else's; and so his daughters would be regarded as more important hearth-wardens than anyone else's. When the kings were abolished, Vesta stayed on; and since there were no king's daughters to serve her, the college of Vestals came into being. First two, then four, and in historic times six maidens served in the temple of Vesta which was close to the Regia or king's house in the Forum. Their own house was next door. The foundations of all three, and a charming restoration of part of the temple, are visible to this day. The temple is round, because it imitates the shape of the first primitive huts of the Latins. The Vestals were girls of good family, and might start their service at the age of seven. After thirty years they might retire, and even marry, though not many of them did. The Vestals were under the direction of the Pontifex Maximus (chief priest) himself. The great antiquity of the cult is shown by the fact that the sacred animal of Vesta was the ass, the Mediterranean animal par excellence, and not the horse, which is Indo-European. The feast of Vesta was held in mid-June, when the temple had its annual clean, the water used being drawn not from the public mains, but from a sacred spring. The asses were garlanded with flowers, and given a holiday.

Strictly speaking the sacred hearth was not a temple, not having been consecrated by the augurs. If the fire went out, the Vestals, after being whipped by the Pontifex Maximus, must rekindle it by rubbing a lucky board with a borer until fire resulted – another proof of the antiquity of the foundation.

Thus we find at the very centre of the Roman liturgy one of its most honoured goddesses venerated in a manner which takes us straight back to the primitive hut and its magic.

Lupercalia

The list of primitive ceremonies is long. One more may be mentioned, because it is familiar to English-speaking readers from its having been incorporated, with great dramatic effect, by Shakespeare in his *Julius Caesar*, namely the *Lupercalia*. The ceremony was extremely complicated, and had evidently taken a long time to evolve. In origin it was, as its name implies, the ritual for keeping off the wolves, *lupi*, which were the chief scourge of the flocks, even (as Virgil reminds us) when they were in the folds, as they would still be on 15 February when the rite was celebrated. Certain young men, chosen probably from two particular families, stripped naked except for a girdle of goat-skin and then, carrying flails of goat-hide in their hands, ran all round the boundaries of the primitive Palatine settlement, thus, as in the *ambarvalia*, making it secure against evil spirits and other aggressors. Why goat-hide? Because the goat is the most aggressive, potent and tough of the smaller domesticated beasts, far more so than a sheep, and therefore of stronger magic against a wolf. As the young athletes progressed – and they too must have been pretty tough to endure naked the rigours of a February day in Rome – they would give a flick, just for good measure, with the goat-flail to any woman they encountered, thereby giving her a dose of this doubly powerful male medicine. And so it came to be believed that 'the barren, touched in this holy chase, shake off their sterile curse'.

Flamen Dialis

Not only the rituals but the priests themselves were surrounded by the primitive, in the form of taboos. Let us take the most august of all (except

for the Pontifex Maximus), the Flamen Dialis, or priest of Jupiter. It happens that by good fortune we still possess a delightful work called *Attic Nights*, written in the middle of the second century A.D. by a certain Aulus Gellius. It recounts table-talk at the university of Athens, and is full of good things. The fifteenth chapter of his tenth book is devoted to describing the numerous rules and regulations which still in his day surrounded the Flamen Dialis. 'It is unlawful for the priest of Jupiter to ride upon a horse, or to look upon the army on parade outside the city boundary; so that he is very rarely elected consul, because wars were entrusted to consuls.' The horse taboo is interesting: it is a parallel to Vesta's preference

for the ass. 'Wars *were* entrusted' – but no longer, for in Gellius' day it was the emperor who alone was permitted to take command of the army; yet the old disqualification still lingered. The flamen might not take an oath. He might not wear a ring, unless it were perforated and without a gem. No fire might be taken from his house except for a sacred rite. If a fettered suppliant entered his house he must be freed, the bonds being drawn up to the roof and thence lowered into the street (to prevent a second defilement of the door?). He had no knot in his headdress, or girdle or in any part of his dress, which must have been decidedly awkward. In his headdress he wore an olive-twig, as we can see in the *Ara Pacis*

sculptures. His barber must be a free man, using bronze shears – no new-fangled iron for so holy a man – and his shorn hair and his nail parings must be buried under a fruitful tree. He must not touch or even name a shegoat, raw flesh, ivy or beans, nor walk beneath a vine arbour. He must eat only unleavened bread. 'For him every day is a holy day.' The feet of his bed must be smeared lightly with clay, he must not sleep out of this bed for three successive nights, and no-one else may sleep in it. At the foot of his bed there must be a box of sacrificial cakes. He might not go out without his cap, though Gellius tells us that by his time, as a concession to human frailty, he was allowed to take it off indoors. He must change his

Top right. The corn supply of Rome was made into an imperial department by Augustus, hence the title 'Annona Augusta'. This coin of the reign of Titus (A.D. 79–81) shows Annona personified as a beneficient deity holding a cornucopia in her left hand and in her right a balance to symbolise the just distribution of corn. As the ship's prow and basket with lotus flowers suggest, Egypt was Rome's main source of corn.

Centre right. Felicitas, a goddess of good luck, was introduced in the second century B.C. by L. Licinius Lucullus. She soon became prominent in official cults and was often referred to in public ceremonies. This copper coin dates from the rein of Antoninus Pius (A.D. 138–161). The letters S.C. denote that it was struck 'Senatus Consulto', the issue of copper coins left to that body by the Emperors.

Right. Fresco of a sacrifice being performed by women as part of the family rituals. Domus Augustana, Rome.

underclothes indoors, because he must not appear naked in the open air, that is in the eye of Jupiter. If his wife, known as the flaminica, dies he abdicates his office, and his marriage can be dissolved only by death – a rare condition in Rome, where divorce was so easy. He never touches a dead body or enters a cemetery. The priestess, says Gellius, was 'about the same', but had some extras of her own. She wore a dyed robe, and when she made her rounds of the district chapels, she might not dress her hair or even comb it, a terrible deprivation for a Roman matron of the second century A.D., when women's coiffures were very elaborate. As a final guarantee of modesty, this lady might not ascend more than three rungs of a ladder, 'except the Greek kind', whatever that may have been.

Life must have been rather constricted for the priest and priestess. Yet the taboos had lasted right down to the days of the Antonines. It is fairly clear that if Roman religion had by that time amounted to no more than these primitive observances, the Romans would have been a good deal poorer, spiritually speaking, than we know them to have been. But before we examine the methods – and they were manifold – by which they endeavoured to escape from their primitive past, it may be well briefly to indicate how religion was organised not only in the family but by the state.

34

The State Cult

Hitherto, religion has been presented as a function of the clan, which had gradually, as in the case of Vesta, spread from the private realm to the public, or, as in the more usual case of the Lupercalia, from the purely magical to the political. It will now be appropriate to discover, if possible, how the state cult became stabilised.

The Roman Calendar

To this end we turn to the state calendars, in which all the public 'days of obligation' were duly recorded. It happens that we possess considerable portions, engraved on stone, of a calendar which, although the fragments date from the late republic to the early empire, do give us the state agenda as they were in the pre-Etruscan days of Numa, after whom the calendar is called. We can also consult another invaluable document, the *Fasti* of Ovid, a poem of 4772 lines in six books, in which month by month and day by day the poet describes the festivals of the first half of the year. He had intended to complete it for the last six months, but never did.

The Roman calendar passed through three distinct stages. First, in the early days, the Romans observed a year of ten months. This does not mean that they divided the year decimally (not even the French revolutionaries did that): it means that they reckoned ten months from March to December, and simply ignored the 'dead' months of January and February. This may strike us as odd, to say the least; but it is in fact fairly common practice among savages, and parallels have been found as far apart as Africa and New Zealand. 'There is

some ground for thinking', says Sir James Frazer in his edition of the *Fasti*, 'that the Anglo-Saxons at one time recognised, or at least named, only ten months of the year: for according to Bede they had only one name for December and January and only one for June and July.' This primitive Roman calendar started with the month of Mars (March), followed by Aprilis from *aperire*, to open, because the earth opens up in that month. Then came May, dedicated to Maia, an ancient goddess, consort perhaps of Vulcan, next June which commemorated the Etruscan deity Uni, or Juno. The remainder were simply numbered, Quintilis and Sextilis, fifth and sixth, followed by September to December, seventh to tenth. Quintilis and Sextilis were replaced in imperial times by July and August in honour of Julius Caesar and Augustus.

Stage two was introduced by the Etruscans, who added January and February, thus bringing the 'dead' months to life. They clearly intended to make January the first month, dedicated to Janus, who as we have seen was the god of entry; but the expulsion of the Etruscan dynasty put a stop to this, and the first of March remained the first day of the year until considerably later – until 153 B.C., in fact. February was dedicated not to Febris goddess of fever, an important deity who had two shrines in Rome, but to Februus who was in later days identified with Dis, the Latin Pluto. February was the month during which the City was purified by appeasing the dead with offerings and sacrifices, called *februalia*. Februus is no more than the personification of this rite.

The month had three fixed lunar points; kalends, the first day; ides, the full moon; and nones midway between, so called because it was the ninth day, counting inclusively from the full moon. The first day was called kalends, or callings, because on that day the pontifices, using an antique formula, called out on the Capitol whether the nones would fall on the seventh or ninth day of the month – a variation imposed by the variation in the length of the months. In effect, the days of the new moon, first quarter, and full moon were observed. The rest of the month, when the moon was waning, and therefore unlucky, had no name at all: you simply reckoned its days by numbering them backwards from the first day of the next month. This clumsy and involved system lasted right down to the end of the Roman world.

Timetable of Festivals

But however rickety the calendar might be, it did introduce for the first time a definite order into the religious practices of the Romans, not merely as heads or members of families, but as Roman citizens. The calendar of Numa can be dated roughly by the fact that it includes the cult of Quirinus on his own hill, the Quirinal, that is, before he had removed to the Capitol, but makes no mention of the Capitoline triad; nor does it make any reference to Diana, the goddess who was brought from Latium and installed on the Aventine before the end of the kingly period.

The calendar itself has two main functions. First, it divides the days of

This calendar was, like all early calendars, lunar. March, May, Quintilis and October had 31 days each, February 28, and the rest 29: total 355. Twelve moons do not add up to one solar year, and so to keep the calendar roughly in tune with the solar year a month was inserted, or intercalated, to use the technical term, from time to time, being placed between the 23rd and 24th February. We now come to the third stage in the development of the Roman, and our own, calendar. The intercalation was so carelessly done that by the time of Julius Caesar (who as Pontifex Maximus was responsible for the calendar) the official year had become three months ahead of the solar. He therefore borrowed an improved calendar from Egypt in the year 46. This is called after him the Julian calendar, and is still in use by certain Eastern Churches. It was amended by Pope Gregory XIII in 1582. This Gregorian calendar (which was in fact available to Julius Caesar in the archives of Alexandria University had he but known it) is the one we now use.

To make matters more complicated, the days of the month were not numbered serially, as they now are.

the month into *fasti* (from *fas*, right) and *nefasti*, that is, days on which business might be transacted and those on which it might not. Secondly it gives us the dates of no less than forty-five festivals. The calendar thus shows the agenda, as it were, of a state still founded on agriculture, but already developing into a community which has legal and political business to transact and wars to wage – a perfect miniature, that is, of the Roman republic which was to be. It is in March and October that we find these traits most strongly marked. In the month of Mars, for instance, up to the 23rd, the Salii, the 'leaping' priests of Mars, performed their dance, brandishing spears and clashing the holy shields called *ancilia*, of which the original was believed to have fallen from heaven. The priests were clad like ancient Latin warriors, and the object of the dance, during which they invoked not only Mars but also Saturn the god of sowing, was twofold, to expel all the evil spirits who had entered the city during the winter, and by their leaping, to stimulate growth through sympathetic magic, for both of which Frazer cites parallels from Africa and Europe.

On the 19th the *ancilia* were lustrated, and on the 23rd the trumpets. On the 14th occurred the second *Equirria*, which means that the horses of the army were being lustrated. Spears, shields, and horses – all the panoply of the host is put into good order and spiritual repair during this month of Mars. There had been a previous *equirria* on 27 February, and that month had also witnessed on the 24th the *Regifugium*, or flight of the king, about which we really know nothing at all, except that, like the Equirria, it was regarded as a festival.

In October the fighting season is

over and a second process of purification must be undertaken. On the 15th, the Ides, there took place a very strange ritual, not mentioned in the calendar, wherein after a chariot race in the Campus Martius the off horse of the winning team was sacrificed to Mars, and its tail cut off and carried by a runner to the Regia, where it was hung up to drip blood onto the altar, while the head was fought over by two rival parties, one drawn from the Via Sacra which ran and still runs through the Forum, and the other from the Subura, a district on the north-east side of the Forum. Neither in antiquity nor in our own day has

Above. The Master Cutler. From an altar erected during the first century A.D. by Lucius Cornelius Atimetus. It displays his wares, which include sickles and pruning-knives for use in the still important countryside. Musei Vaticani.

Opposite. This statue of Mars of the seventh century B.C. is markedly Etruscan in style. As usual in Greek statues the left foot is to the fore. Mars god of war, not to be identified with the Greek Ares, was originally a spirit of vegetation. He ranks next to Jupiter; and was the object of much ceremonial honour during his month of March. Museo Archeologico, Florence.

any meaning been found for this gruesome rite; but as the blood was used by the Vestals for purifications and the horse is often held to personify the corn-spirit, Rose conjectures that here again we may have a survival from primitive agricultural magic. On the 19th occurred the Armilustrium, which is self-explanatory, and on the same day the Salii, who had again been active in the earlier part of the month, laid up their shields to signify that the campaigning season was over.

Thus, as Warde Fowler points out, the calendar shows both political and military development. But its chief

Above left. Ceres, an ancient Latin goddess of vegetation. After the introduction, at the behest of the Sibylline books, of Demeter, together with Dionysos, in 496 B.C., Ceres became completely identified with and submerged in her.

Above centre. Pomona, Milton's 'with fruits Pomona crowned', was the goddess in charge of them. She, like Flora, had her own flamen. Ovid makes her the wife of Vertumnus, the god who like herself is linked with the return of the seasons and the fertility of the earth. Galleria degli Uffizi, Florence.

Above right. Flora was the goddess of 'all that flourishes'. She had her own priest – one of the twelve flamens said to have been instituted by Numa. Her festivals were called Floralia. Courtesans took part in them, whence Flora became a popular name with these ladies.

Opposite above left. Glaucus was a sea god, whom Virgil makes the father of the Sybil of Cumae. He designed the *Argo* and fought alongside the Argonauts.

Opposite above right. Saturn was a very ancient Italian deity later identified with Cronos. His reign over Latium was regarded as a Golden Age. In imperial times in Punic regions Saturn was also identified with Baal.

Left. Father Tiber with his oar, his horn of plenty, a rather crushed-looking wolf and twins to identify him. The Romans liked river statues; there is another Tiber, coupled with a Nile, on the Campidoglio.

emphasis is on agriculture which was the basis of the life of the people. March, as we have seen, was devoted predominantly to military preparations. April is more concerned with agriculture. On the 15th at the Fordicidia a pregnant cow was sacrificed to Tellus, the Earth-goddess, and the unborn calf burned, probably to secure the fertility of the crops. On the 19th the Cerealia seems to have had the same object in view. On the 21st came the Parilia, or Palilia, in honour of Pales, a rustic god so old that he preceded the foundation of Rome. The rite was a lustration of cattle before they left their winter pastures for the wilder runs of the hills, comparable to the lustration of an army before it left for a campaign. It was held that Rome was founded on that day, and so 21 April was kept as the birthday of Rome. It still is.

On the 23rd the Vinalia sought protection for the vines, and on the 25th, when the ear was beginning to form, the evil Robigus was formally propitiated.

May was a comparatively slack season, because the precautions taken in April were considered adequate for

Above. The Ponte Rotto. In 179 B.C. the two censors built a bridge with stone foundations. In 142 the then censors gave the bridge stone arches, and it thus became the first all-stone bridge in Rome. It is the vestiges of that bridge, often ruined and restored and finally abandoned in 1598, that we now see. Of Rome's twenty-one road bridges, four are still wholly or in part the gift of ancient Rome. An arch of one of them, the Ponte Cestio, is visible in the background.

Opposite above. The three high deities of the Capitol were Jupiter, Minerva and Juno. Here they are depicted in a relief. Museo Nazionale Romano, Rome.

Opposite below. The Pomerium was the line demarcating an augurally constituted city. The boundary was marked by ritual ploughing, as shown in this relief.

Right. Fides Publica, the personification of good faith. Her cult is very old, said to have been founded by Numa. Coin of Domitian (A.D. 81–96). Museo Nazionale Romano, Rome.

the safeguarding of the growing crops, but at the end of the month, the whole of what was called the *ager Romanus*, or state domain, was lustrated by the Arval Brethren, whose office was to bring fertility to the fields. This was a movable feast depending on the weather, and so does not appear in the calendar. Meanwhile, on 14 or 15 May, a solemn procession had visited the twenty-seven chapels in the city called Argei, whence they collected straw puppets which had probably been deposited there two months earlier, twenty-seven in number, because twenty-seven is thrice nine, and so of powerful magical significance. These puppets were carried by the pontiffs and the Vestals and the praetors, followed by the citizens 'who may lawfully attend rites' to the Pons Sublicius, the wooden bridge below the Palatine which until the building of the so-called *ponte rotto* by Aemilius in 179 B.C. was the only link between the two banks. (It was this bridge that Horatius defended 'in the brave days of old'.) Then after sacrifice, the puppets were cast into the Tiber. The ancients were as much in the dark as we are about the meaning of the ceremony. Some thought the puppets were surrogates for human sacrifices, others that they represented men over sixty years of age who in the good old days were thrown from the bridge

to drown. Plutarch says this was 'the greatest of purifications', from which Frazer suggests that the object of the rite was to sweep out to sea all the evils which had accumulated during the past year; and he quotes parallels. 'But', he adds, 'there is another and simpler explanation of the Argei which deserves to be considered. May they not be offerings to the river-god, to pacify him, and to induce him to put up with the indignity of having a bridge built across his stream? . . . We can easily imagine the indignation which a river-god must feel at the sight of a bridge, and of people passing dryshod across it, who in the course of nature would have been drowned at the ford. Thus the deity is robbed of his prey; and he naturally puts in a claim for compensation. . . . On this hypothesis, nothing could be more fitting than that the offering should be under the auspices of the pontiffs, whose very name, signifying "bridge-makers", marked them out as the culprits responsible for the sacrilege, and therefore as the penitents bound to atone for it.'

In June the chief task was, as already explained, the cleaning of the *penus* of Vesta, so as to be ready to receive the grain of the new crop. July brought a group of festivals so obscure that it is profitless to examine them. Harvest festivals proper begin in August: the Consualia on the 21st

and the Opiconsiva on the 25th both have affinities with the word *condere*, to lay together, and seem to relate to the storing of the new crop. In between came the Volcanalia on the 23rd, to ward off rick-burning or accidental fires which are most likely to occur in the hot dry weather of late summer.

Thereafter for the rest of the year there was nothing to do but plough and sow, operations which were not regarded as being liable to malignant influences, or at any rate to none which Mother Earth could not deal with, and so they leave no trace in the calendar. But when the autumn sowing was over, on 17 December the *Saturnalia* was celebrated, Saturnus being connected with the root meaning 'sow', flanked by a second consualia on the 15th and an Opalia on the 19th. The Saturnalia is (or are, the word is plural) familiar to us, because the term has passed into our own language, and for a reason which illustrates the way in which most of the other rites we have mentioned lost their original force and meaning, without falling wholly into desuetude. The majority relate to agriculture, the occupation and livelihood of a rural society; but what did they mean to an urban community which had for generations lived on imported corn, until by the time of the late republic this imported corn was

actually given away? 'Bread and cir-
cuses' had by then become the prer-
ogative of the mob, and farming was
forgotten. But the Saturnalia was still
celebrated – and it survived right up
to the end of paganism – as a jolly
winter festival. People had long forgotten that it had any connection at
all with sowing; just as thousands
who celebrate Christmas as a holiday
(it inherited its festive garb from the
Saturnalia) would no longer associate
it with the birth of Jesus Christ in
Bethlehem.

It is time therefore to say farewell
to the agricultural origins of the
Roman cult, bearing in mind as we
do so that it was this farming cycle

Above and top. Children at play, from a
Roman sarcophagus now in the Vatican,
are portrayed here with realism and
affection.

Opposite. A Roman kitchen, bakery and
cellar, with a simple banquet. This type of
relief is typical of the direct and down-to-
earth Romans. It is quite un-Greek.

Below. Roman funeral. The Romans
practised both inhumation and cremation:
in imperial times inhumation in
magnificent sarcophagi became common.
This scene shows (top left) the widow
and her servants, then an image of the
deceased, now gathered to the stars (note
the star and crescent), more mourners,
horn and trumpet-player. Below, bearers
and flute-players. Museo d'Arte Nazionale
d'Abrazzo L'Aquila.

that gave Rome its first formal
religion. We find, in short, that Rome
had come to worship four superior
gods, who from the ceremonies devoted to them have come to acquire
personalities, namely Janus, Jupiter,
Mars and Quirinus, and one goddess,
Vesta. Each of the four gods had a
personal priest: the *Rex sacrorum*,
successor of the kings and as at Athens charged only with the former
kings' sacred functions, who lived at
the Regia, looked after Janus; and the
other three had their own flamens. Of
the host of lesser *numina* some of the
more important have already been
mentioned. Nine of them had flamens
of their own, Volcanus, Furrina,

Portunus, Pales, Flora, Pomona, Carmenta and Falacer. Of these, Falacer is wholly unknown, Furrina and Volturnus almost so. Of Carmenta all we know is that her priestesses cast the fortunes of children at their birth. It is Saint Augustine who tells us this, so she must have survived until his day. No new flamens were appointed until the introduction of Caesarworship.

To sum up: we have now reached a stage where the religion of the primitive farming community, directed to the promotion of agriculture and its protection from enemies seen and unseen, surrounded by magic and hedged by taboos, has advanced suf-

Above. Roman butcher's shop, conducted in a thoroughly Roman way. The joints are displayed in an orderly manner, the scales are handy for weighing them, and the master is keeping the tally in his ledger.

Below. Relief of a Roman shop. Scavi di Ostia.

ficiently to be crystallised into calendars, to be served by a regular priesthood, and to be provided with the festivals and sanctions of an urban state. This was a great step forward; but as Warde Fowler points out, there were serious drawbacks to this religion of the *Di Indigetes*, the native gods as they were called, to distinguish them from the newcomers

who were about to arrive. 'Most prominent among these was the fact that it was the religion of the state as a whole and not of the individual or family. . . . At Rome, though the earliest traces and traditions of law show a certain consecration of morality, in as much as the criminal is made over as a kind of propitiatory sacrifice to the deity he has offended, yet in the ordinary course of life, so far as I can discern, the individual was left very much where he was, before the state arose, in his relation to the Divine.'

Some of the new arrivals, it is true, would be introduced into the state cult, but others were to be the harbingers of personal religion.

The Newcomers

As has been explained earlier, Roman religion, by the beginning of the Republic, had become crystallised but not yet fossilised. That is to say, it was now a highly organised state cult, in the hands of special officers. The individual as such took no part in the 'services': all that was left to him were the primitive rites of home and farm. Progressively, with the development of an urban civilisation, these rites became inadequate for the spiritual needs of the ordinary citizen. Moreover, through commerce, through warfare and through travel in search of enlightenment the Roman citizen became increasingly familiar with, and attracted to, the religions and philosophies of other nations. These 'other nations' may be classified in four categories: the Italians, the Etruscans, the Greeks and the peoples of the Orient.

Heracles

The process of adoption from without had begun even before the birth of the Republic. The advent of Minerva has already been mentioned. It used to be held that Minerva was an Etruscan deity; it is now generally believed that she was Italian. From Italy also two important Greek cults, those of Heracles and of Castor and Pollux, the Dioskouroi, had reached Rome at a very early period, having come from Latin towns with Greek commercial connections. (So often religion goes hand in hand with trade.) Indeed, they mark the first, if indirect, contact of Rome and Greece. Heracles made the same sort of appeal in antiquity as the 'strong man' does in contemporary fiction or entertainment: he was, although a demigod, a human sort of creature, fond of wine and women, but superhuman in his ability to avoid the consequences of indulging in those hobbies. Heracles, latinised as Hercules, was first established at Tibur (Tivoli) where he seems to have protected traders, and was thence brought to Rome.

Castor and Pollux

The cult of Castor and Pollux came from Tusculum, the lovely hilltop above Frascati where Cicero had one of his villas. Traditionally it was introduced in 499 B.C., when the Heavenly Twins appeared in the Forum to

The columns of the portico of the Temple of Castor and Pollux in the Roman Forum. They date from A.D. 6 and are made of the famous Paros marble.

Next to the so-called temple of Fortuna Virilis is this graceful building, wrongly styled the temple of Vesta, because its circular shape recalls that in the Forum. It is of the Augustan age, or perhaps a little earlier. It stands near the old port, for up to the nineteenth century the Tiber was a waterway, and some think it may have been dedicated to Portumnus, but this is a mere conjecture. The Romans liked round temples modelled on the Greek *tholos*. There is one at Tivoli from which Soane copied his Tivoli corner in the Bank of England.

announce the victory of Lake Regillus, where they had fought on the side of the Romans against the Latins and Tarquins, and had then brought the good news to Rome. They watered their winged steeds at the *Lacus Juturnae* in the Forum, and so in 484 a temple was erected in their honour. The *lacus*, a rectangular stone cistern, is still there, as well as three surviving columns of the temple as rebuilt for the third time by Augustus. The Twins too, were associated with commerce, and a weights and measures office was attached to their shrine.

The Etruscans
Etruscan influences had for long been at work on Roman religion, and it was through the Etruscans that the Romans received most of their first intimations of Greek religion and philosophy. They therefore possess a double importance in the evolution of Rome's religious experience.

Whether the first Etruscans were immigrants from Asia, or were sprung from a mixture of Villanovan and neolithic stock, it is clear that they very early came within the ambit of Greek ideas. Their tombs have yielded not only artefacts that show Greek influence, but some of the most beautiful Greek vases in existence.

Given their close contact with, and one-time dominance of, Rome, it would be easy for them to pass on these Greek ideas to the community on the south bank of the Tiber. What is interesting to us is that the Romans were discerning enough to adopt only what they thought was useful. Etruscan tomb paintings contain examples of what the *Cambridge Ancient History*, (Vol. viii, p. 449) calls a 'demon-haunted religious consciousness'. 'No sign of this religion of terror', says the same authority, 'reappears in Roman literature or art. . . . The fear of punishment after death, against which Lucretius wrote is a far more sober thing, derived directly from Greek sources. It is significant again that there is not found in the Roman hierarchy a single deity of purely Etruscan origin'. What the Romans did adopt from the Etruscans were two things: the building of temples and much, if not all, of their rites of divination.

At first sight the building of temples seems a harmless enough innovation, an improvement even on temporary altars of turf set up on some hallowed spot, either in the open or sheltered by an open rustic roof. From the purely aesthetic point of view it was; but once a temple had been built it

was only natural that a representation of the deity should be placed within it. Thus the Roman *numina* became personified. No longer were they spirits: they had become graven images. 'For more than 170 years', says Varro (first century B.C.) quoted by Saint Augustine, 'the Romans worshipped their gods without images (*simulacra*)', that is from the foundation of the city until the time of the first Etruscan king. The earliest Roman temple to which we can assign even an approximate date was the great temple on the Capitol. It is said to have been begun under the Tarquins and to have been dedicated in the first year of the Republic, that is in 509 B.C. It was built in the Etruscan style, with foundations of Etruscan masonry. It was dedicated to the triad Jupiter, Juno and Minerva, and inside was a statue of Jupiter. Thus the trend from animism to anthropomorphism, the making of gods in man's image, was accelerated. It would take centuries for the process to be reversed, after bitter struggles led by Greek philosophy and Judaeo-Christian theology. Well might Varro say that 'those who first made images of the gods for the nations both removed fear from their states and added error'. The Roman ceased to fear his gods because representation of them in the round bred familiarity, which in its turn bred contempt: Roman discipline based on religious sanctions was eroded. Error was added because the *numen* was capable of spiritual development whereas a statue is not.

Augurs

The other department of Roman religion to be formulated or at least systematised by the Etruscans was divination. Under the Republic, the college of Augurs, as they were called, ranked with the *Pontifices* as the repositories of Roman religious lore. The origin of the college is ascribed to Romulus, and after 300 B.C., it numbered nine members. Whether the word *augur* is derived from the root *av* meaning bird or from the same root as Augustus is still debated, but it is certain that augury in its later development owed much to Etruscan influence, and that it depended on birds. Ovid tells us that Romulus and Remus decided which was to be the founder of Rome by bird-watching. Throughout the history of the Republic we constantly read of the importance of birds. It is expressed in Ovid's line: '*magna fides avium est, experiamur aves*' – 'great faith is put in birds, let us try the birds'. The way they ate, the way they drank, or refused to, where they perched, what sounds they made – from such indications the will of heaven could be deduced, for is not the sky their natural habitat? The Etruscans' special contribution to the augurs' craft was the art of divination by the inspection of the entrails of victims. The first part of a handbook called *Disciplina Etrusca* deals with the subject; and it was practised by *haruspices*, whom the Romans called in from Etruria when needed. Another skill of the Etruscans was the interpretation of lightning, both by day and by night.

The object of divination, whether by augury or by other means, was not so much to foretell the future as to ensure that the gods were favourable to the enterprise about to be undertaken – part of the general 'My will be done' attitude of Roman religion. Since it is not possible to guarantee

that a favourable omen will be forthcoming just when it is needed, this contingency was provided for by two recognised evasions, (a) a bad omen has no force for anyone who denies having seen it – i.e. the augur could turn a blind eye on it, on the principle that what the eye does not see the heart will not grieve for, and (b) it is the *report* of the omen that counts, so that the augur could always, if he chose to and were of the same political persuasion, give the magistrate the assurance he sought. It is obvious that this equivocal mumbo-jumbo, which remained in vogue throughout the days of the Republic, must have been a corrupting influence on Roman religion: it encouraged superstition and was a perpetual temptation to manipulate religion for political ends.

How cynically the upper class Roman regarded it may be inferred from some instances cited by Livy. As early as the year 293, he tells us, in the last struggle against the Samnites, one of the chicken-keepers, (*pullarii*) had reported to the consul that the fowls had given a good omen in their eating. The consul's nephew, 'a young man born before people were taught to despise the gods', knew that they had not, and told his uncle. The consul merely replied that it had been reported to him as a good omen, and that therefore it was 'a splendid augury for the Roman people and army'. Just to make sure, though, the chicken-keeper was put in the forefront of the battle: he was killed.

A little later, in 249, P. Claudius Pulcher and his colleague Junius both neglected the warning of the *pullarius* (although Junius' cognomen was Pullus), and both were defeated at sea. Claudius is even said to have had the birds thrown into the water, saying that if they wouldn't eat, they could drink instead. Flaminius, the consul who was defeated by Hannibal at Lake Trasimene in 217 had left Rome with all his religious duties unperformed. Marcellus, his famous and successful contemporary, though himself an accomplished augur, refused to be guided by the electric sparks which appeared at the tips of

his soldiers' spears, and played safe by always travelling with the blinds of his litter drawn, to avoid seeing evil omens.

The year 193 was marked by a succession of earthquakes so continuous that the Senate could not meet and all public business was suspended, the consuls being almost uninterruptedly occupied with ceremonies of expiation. The Sibylline books were consulted and the prescribed remedies applied. Finally, in exasperation the consuls, urged by the Senate, proclaimed that one earthquake a day was enough, and that if on a day appointed for the expiation of one earthquake another occurred it was not to be reported; which moves Livy to remark that the Romans had evidently grown tired not only of earthquakes but of expiatory ceremonies as well.

Superciliousness and superstition, both enemies of true religion, were thus fostered together. To quote the summing-up of the *Cambridge Ancient History*: 'The influence of the Etruscans was less than has sometimes been supposed, but in these two respects, the encouragement of anthropomorphism through the introduction of temples and temple statues, and the superstitious elaboration of divination, it had a lasting and deteriorating effect.'

Dei Consentes

It was from the Etruscans that the Romans borrowed another element of their state cult, not open to the same criticism as the foregoing, but equally important in its development, namely the *Dei Consentes*, or consenting gods. The Etruscans recognised twelve deities, six male and six female, with mysterious names, who assisted Jupiter in coming to important decisions, specially in the matter of launching thunderbolts, rather like a modern Defence Council. The Romans took over these gods, but they identified them with the twelve great gods of the Hellenic pantheon. Thus it came about that we have the familiar, and sometimes confusing, assimilation of Greek and Roman, as follows:

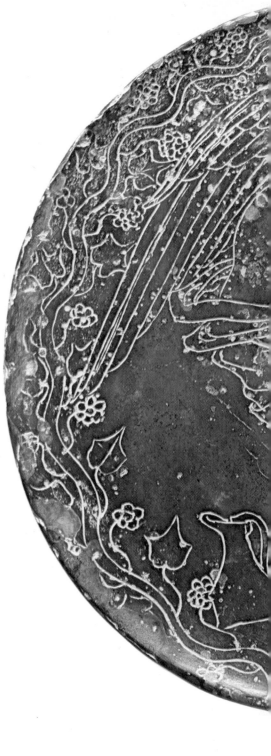

Left. The Apollo of Veii, a life-sized Etruscan terracotta statue, *c.* 500 B.C. It belongs to a group representing Hercules' theft of the holy hind of the god Apollo at Delphi which decorated a temple at Veii. Museo Nazionale di Villa Giulia, Rome.

Above. The back of an Etruscan mirror depicting an augur examining entrails. Because of the association between birds and foretelling the future this augur wears wings. Musei Vaticani.

Male
Jupiter – Zeus
Neptune – Poseidon
Mars – Ares
Apollo – Apollo
Vulcan – Hephaistos
Mercury – Hermes

Female
Juno – Hera
Minerva – Athena
Diana – Artemis
Venus – Aphrodite
Vesta – Hestia
Ceres – Demeter

Once the identifications were made, Roman gods and goddesses became ever more anthropomorphic, because all the legends of their Greek counterparts now became their own property.

Apollo and the Sybil of Cumae

In the foregoing catalogue only one god is common to both sides, or rather belongs to one side only and has no counterpart, and that is Apollo, the most attractive and inspiring of all ancient deities. The reason for this is that he was borrowed very early from the Greeks not of Magna Graecia in the as yet remote deep south, but from the Greek colony of Cumae at the northern tip of the Bay of Naples. Cumae was famous for the worship of Apollo, and was at the same time the seat of a Sybil, or prophetess of Apollo.

The original Sybil was a Trojan maiden of noble birth – according to one story that is, for there were as so often a number to choose from. The Romans preferred the Trojan legend because, in order to keep up with the Greeks, who went back to Homer if not beyond, they liked to maintain that they were descended from princely Trojan refugees of whom the chief was Aeneas. The Sybils were endowed by Apollo with the gift of prophecy; and one of the most prominent of them established herself at Erythrae, on the coast of Asia Minor near Chios. It was this very prophetess, so tradition held, who had migrated to Cumae, where she died at a very great age in circumstances

which are variously related. Some say that Apollo decreed that she might live for as many years as she could hold grains of sand in her hand on condition that she never again saw Erythrae; but one day she received a letter from home which the Erythraeans had thoughtlessly sealed with the earth of Erythrae. The Sybil died on the spot. Others hold that Apollo offered her not only long life but perpetual youth at the price of her virginity. She refused, and as she aged became smaller and smaller, until finally she was no bigger than a grasshopper, and was hung up in a cage at Cumae. 'What do you want?' the children would ask her. 'I want to die' was the answer.

The Sybil of Cumae was to become immortal because it is she who in the sixth book of Virgil's epic introduces Aeneas to the underworld. But her influence on Roman destiny had started long before. It was she, men believed, who had sold to king Tarquin, after much haggling and rejection, three – at three times the price of the nine she had first offered – oracular books, the Sibylline oracles. Perhaps originally the officers in charge of these matters – first two, later ten – journeyed to Cumae to consult the resident oracle when need arose, and the compilation, preserved in the temple of Capitoline Jupiter, was made later. In any case the beginning of Sibylline influence in Roman affairs must be dated in the year 493, when during a famine the oracle enjoined the building of a temple to Ceres, Liber and Libera below the Aventine – in reality, a shrine to the Greek triad Demeter, Iacchos and Persephone, Iacchos being the son either of Demeter or Persephone, or

even the husband of Demeter. The introduction of this triad is of prime importance, because it introduces Rome to Eleusis, the setting of the most famous of all Greek mysteries, into which emperors would be proud to be initiated, and of which Iacchos was the torchbearer and procession-leader.

The Sibyl of Cumae, whose grotto-chapel still echoes awesomely to those who visit it, having brought off this 'coup', as it may well be styled for it introduced Rome to Greek mysticism, would from time to time, when it seemed that the old gods had failed, advise that other Greek deities be introduced. It was thus, for instance, that Hermes and Poseidon, already mentioned, arrived in Rome. Another was the Greek god of healing, Asklepios, a son of Apollo, who became Romanised as Aesculapius.

Hercules and the Twins were worshipped within the city, but the later newcomers were housed outside the *pomœrium*, or official boundary, until the time of the Hannibalic war, thus preserving the distinction between the *di indigetes*, native gods, and the *di novensides*, or newcomers, all of whom had cult-statues and were worshipped in the Greek manner, with head uncovered: Roman celebrants officiated with heads veiled.

New Religious Practices

In 399 during a pestilence, a new form of worship was introduced, which brought the populace into participation. The Sybilline books ordered a *lectisternium*: for eight days the images of three pairs of latinised Greek gods were displayed reclining on couches, with tables of food and drink before them. This was a pleas-

ant innovation: outdoor celebrations are always attractive. Later, yet another popular exercise was introduced, the *supplicatio*, when the citizens, women and children included, wearing wreaths and carrying branches of laurel, like Greek suppliants, went the round of the temples, offering prayers or thanksgivings as occasion might require. The *lectisternium* and *supplicatio* could be combined: the object of both ceremonies was to allow the people some initiative in what had hitherto been the province of priests only.

The Hannibalic, or Second Punic, War of 218-201, 'the war of a man against a nation' as it has been called, marks a turning-point in the history of Roman religion. Amid the disasters and tensions of warfare it seemed to the Roman people that the old *jus*

Above. Roman augury was systematised on Etruscan models. Two Etruscan augurs are shown in this tomb fresco from Tarquineia.

Left. Mercurius, or Mercury, who as his name suggests, protects merchants, and travellers. He was assimilated to Hermes, messenger of the gods. He carries a caduceus or wand, and wears a broad hat and winged sandals. In this version, the wings have been transferred to his head and the sandals discarded. Galleria degli Uffizi.

Right. Antrum of the Sibylline shrine at Cumae where the faithful gathered to obtain prophecies. These were delivered in the form of verse and very often were deliberately ambiguous.

Opposite. Roman temple. This shrine, not far from the Ponte Rotto, is erroneously known as that of Fortuna Virilis. It is a rare example of Graeco-Italian architecture of the Republican era, having been built about 100 B.C. It is typically Roman (a) for being erected on a podium and (b) for having the pillars of the colonnade engaged with the wall of the *cella*. In A.D. 871 it became a church, St Mary of Egypt, and was later used by the Armenian community.

divinum, the state liturgy, had failed to maintain the *pax deorum*, the favour of the gods manifested in peace. Some new, more drastic medicine must be tried to ensure that 'my will be done'. Once again the Sibylline books were consulted, and once again they suggested innovations on Greek lines. Already in 349 the Books had ordained the institution of *ludi scenici*, or pageants, as an antidote to a pestilence. Now, in 217, after the crushing defeat at Lake Trasimene, special 'games' were added to the Roman ones. These exhibitions, in which gladiators no doubt took part, were intended to divert the public mind. Gladiators perpetuated the typically barbarous Etruscan custom of killing slaves on their master's grave. They were originally exhibited at funerals only, the idea being that instead of killing men like brutes, it was more civilised to watch them kill each other like men. Gladiators were first seen in Rome in the year 264 B.C.

An even more barbarous and horrible expiation, also no doubt of Etruscan origin, was resorted to, namely the burying alive in the Forum Boarium (where the gladiators had first been exhibited) of a Greek man and woman and a Gallic man and woman. Livy is justly disgusted by this, 'hardly Roman' he calls it; and yet as we know from the elder Pliny, a writer of the first century A.D. the dreadful custom had continued down to his own day: he had witnessed it and records the prayer which was recited over the victims.

The public mind was also distracted by phenomena which to the very end of Roman history abound in a manner which we find it extremely difficult to grasp, namely prodigies. These might range from a hail of pebbles, not uncommon in a volcanic country, or a rain of blood, red sand brought by the scirocco from the deserts of Africa, to statues falling flat on their faces, from animals with two heads to birds with no livers. Anything in fact, whether ordinary or extraordinary, could be and habitually was regarded as a prodigy, and as such a premonitory occurrence. Sober writers like Plutarch, who was a

Above. Kneeling Venus. This type of statue became highly popular in the Hellenistic and Roman epochs, because the sculptor makes the goddess use her hands to draw attention to those parts of her body which she affects to hide. Musei Vaticani.

Opposite left. Hestia. This imposing statue is of the fifth century B.C., and is now in the Antiquarium Communale at Rome. Hestia was the goddess of the hearth. She never moved from Olympus. She also obtained from Zeus the gift of perpetual virginity. For these two reasons she plays no part in Greek legend. Vesta was assimilated to her.

Opposite right. The western ambulatory of the Temple of Apollo at Pompeii, with a statue of the god. Apollo was the most attractive of all Greek and Roman deities. He is the only one to appear under the same name in both the Greek and Roman pantheon. The reason is that he came to Rome not from Magna Graecia, but, much earlier, from Cumae, on the northern tip of the Bay of Naples, which was also the abode of the Sibyl.

Pages 58–9. Isola Tiberina. This delightful island, 300 metres long and 80 wide, resembles a cargo-ship in outline. It was dedicated to Aesculapius (Asklepios) the god of healing whose cult was introduced into Rome in 201 B.C. It still houses a hospital. Its site, washed by the running water of the river and its abundant fresh air must have commended its therapeutic qualities to the dwellers in the foetid overbuilt alleys of Rome.

Above. The Sibyl of Cumae, as depicted by Michelangelo on the vault of the Sistine Chapel (1508–1512). The Sibyl had been adopted by Christianity, and the first verse of the *Dies Irae* runs: 'Day of wrath, that dreadful day: Heaven and Earth shall burn away/David and the Sybil say'.

Above centre. Diana, the Virgin huntress, assimilated with Artemis. This famous statue, which is known as the Versailles Diana, is probably a copy of a fourth century B.C. original, possibly the work of Leochares.

Above right. Cupid was assimilated with Eros, son of Aphrodite. This statue of him is a copy of one by Lysippus (fourth century B.C.). Museo del Palazzo dei Conservatori, Rome.

Opposite above. Roman gods were often on the move, either for a *lectisternium*, or being carried to the Circus for the games. When they went out, this was the sort of carriage in which they travelled. From a relief in the British Museum, London.

Right. This fresco is of particular interest. It shows a group of children sacrificing to Diana. It underlines the Roman love of children. It also brings to mind the unique group of miniature statues of little girls, devotees of Artemis, recently recovered from Brauron, the celebrated shrine of Artemis in Attica. Musei Vaticani.

Opposite below. Cybele, the Great Goddess, who by command of the Sibylline Books was introduced into Rome in 204 B.C. She is generally represented, as in this statue in the Naples National Museum, as crowned with towers and accompanied by lions.

philosopher, or Ammianus, who was a soldier, regularly give lists of prodigies, with the object of helping us to understand better the events which followed. 'Now the prodigies which accompanied his birth were as follows' – the phrase is familiar to all readers of Roman historians. In fact towards the end of the Roman empire an author actually compiled a Book of Prodigies, which is intended to be a handbook of Roman chronology.

Burying alive and prodigies – it is clear that the Romans were losing their nerve, their *gravitas* or sense of dignity and discipline. But two forward-looking innovations were to come. First, the magistrates ordered a combined *lectisternium* and *supplicatio*, in which twelve gods, Greek and Roman, were displayed side by side. Thus for the first time the distinction between 'native' and 'foreign' gods was obliterated, and Greek ritual applied to both. This decision was indeed a turning-point in the history of Roman worship: henceforth the religion of Rome was to be not Roman but Graeco-Roman.

The Great Mother

Then in 205 came a departure so radical that it is hard to account for it, even given the link between the Sibyl and Asia, except by admitting that oriental influences both on Greece and on Rome had already become far stronger than we might suppose. After an unusually heavy hail of pebbles, the Books, when consulted for the last time in that year, gave the amazing answer that Hannibal, who though defeated was still at large in southern Italy, would leave the country if the Great Mother were brought to Rome. Now the Great Mother was Asiatic. She was worshipped at Pessinus in Galatia, not far from modern Ankara. Sure enough, in April of the following year, the Great Mother, or Cybele as she was known, arrived in Rome, in the guise of a black aerolith, the hallowed stone having been kindly released by king Attalus I of Pergamum, who had decided, rightly, that so far as he was concerned, it was more prudent to keep on the right side of Rome than of Cybele. The oracle of Delphi had supported

Above. This famous fresco in Pompeii shows an initiation into Dionysiac mysteries. Brides are being admitted in what are clearly tense episodes. The figure on the left is that of Silenus-Satyr, often represented as wild, coarse and drunk. But here Silenus is 'dignified, inspired and musical'. (*Oxford Classical Dictionary*, p. 797).

Opposite. Liber Pater (or Dionysos) with his consort Libera. The god of fertility and wine, his feast was celebrated largely in the country and was the occasion for wearing masks, for crude songs and unrestrained merrymaking. From Djemila, Algeria, second or third century, A.D.

the idea and so had the great Scipio himself.

When the goddess arrived at Ostia, the port of Rome, Scipio went on board to receive her, and she was then carried in the arms of Rome's noblest matrons, proud of this visible proof of their connection with the land of Troy, to the Palatine where it was placed in the temple of Victory. The day, 4 April, was thenceforth celebrated as a holiday, on which were

Opposite above. Bacchantes worshipping their god in the form of a bull. Musei Vaticani.

Opposite below left. The satyrs gradually lost their goatish attributes, and became wholly human. But they retained their hedonistic qualities, like this young dancer. Musée du Louvre, Paris.

Opposite below right. This old woman is a Bacchus-addict. She is clutching the wine-jar from which she has for so long drawn comfort. The statue is believed to be copied from a bronze by Miron, who worked in the second half of the third century B.C. Museo del Palazzo dei Conservatori, Rome.

Right. Dionysos, latinised as Bacchus, is generally represented as the ever-young god of wine and jollity, the Liberator, who brought to the west all the joys of the east. He found his way to Rome shortly after the Great Mother, by way of prisoners of war from Etruria or Magna Graecia. The Senate proscribed the Bacchanalia, but Bacchus had come to stay. This relief from Herculaneum shows him with his usual attributes, the pine-cone tipped thyrsus, and the panther, on which he is sometimes shown riding. Museo Archeologico Nazionale, Naples.

Above. Venus, an ancient Roman *numen* later identified with Aphrodite, whose traditional birthplace, as she arose from the waves is near Paphos in Cyprus, shown here.

Opposite. Hermes, with whom the Roman Mercury is generally assimilated. This famous and beautiful statue of the celestial messenger resting comes from the Villa of the Papyri at Herculaneum. It is now in the National Archaeological Museum at Naples. Antique bronzes are rare, because the Middle Agers had lost the skill of smelting the necessary ores, and so any available bronze object was cast into the melting-pot. Museo Archeologico Nazionale, Naples.

Right. Dionysos. The Birth of Dionysos as represented in this sardonyx cameo in a gold mount from Tunis. British Museum, London.

67

Above. Dionysos could be serious, as shown in this bronze head from Herculaneum.

Above left. Silenus, as shown in this bronze from Pompeii, was permanently drunk.

Opposite above. How elegant a Dionysiac celebration could be is proved by this delightful terracotta from Cerveteri. Two satyrs, with fawnskins thrown over their shoulders, (as in Euripides' *Bacchae*) are dancing to the music of a young flautist, while a companion brings in a basket of grapes. They are celebrating the vintage.

Left.Triumph of Bacchus. Dionysus to whom Bacchus was assimilated, came from the Orient, as Euripides among others, declares. He was a jolly god, as represented here, with his leopards and musical accompaniment. Also conflated with Liber, the liberator from inhibitions. Musée Archéologique, Sousse.

Below. The rape of Proserpine (or Persephone) by Pluto is a subject which has attracted poets and artists from Ovid onwards. This fantastically virtuoso and theatrical group was done by Gian Lorenzo Bernini in 1622, when he was twenty-four. Galleria Borghese, Rome.

Above. This epicene statue of Attis, his manhood gone, comes from Ostia. Attis was the partner of the Great Mother. The 'radiate crown' suggests a connection with Mithraism, to which the religion of the Great Mother did in fact make some syncretic contribution. Musei Vaticani.

performed the *Ludi Megalenses, megale* being the feminine form of the Greek adjective meaning great. Aristocratic families, again with their Trojan descent in mind, formed guilds which were placed under the patronage of the protectress of their 'motherland'. The next year, just as had been forecast by the Books, Hannibal did leave Italy, never to return.

The Great Mother was the first eastern deity to be introduced into Rome and the last to be introduced by the Sibylline Books. With her came her partner Attis and his devotees. At the time few Romans, probably, knew about the orgiastic goings-on conducted by self-castrated priests, which constituted their joint cult; but they soon found out, and a resolution of the Senate forbade any Roman citizen to take part in them. Only twenty years later the Senate had to proscribe the Bacchanalia, which had reached Rome through the medium of prisoners taken in the war from Etruria or Magna Graecia, and had spread

alarmingly among the young. The Senate not only forbade Bacchus-worship in Rome, but took the unprecedented and high-handed action of compelling her Latin allies to enforce a similar ban.

These repressions may have had some immediate effect; but the barriers were down. In future it would be from the East, from Asia and from Egypt that the chief stimuli of Roman religion would come, culminating in the arrival of Judaism and Christianity, both of them eastern religions in origin. The populace might find in eastern emotionalism the release and relief they increasingly sought; but Greece was to give one more gift to Rome. The assimilation of Roman deities to their Greek counterparts led not only to the appropriation of Greek legend and myth, so that the absence of Roman myth was largely overcome, but it turned Roman minds to Greek philosophy. Greek philosophy was to become the religion of the educated Roman.

Educated Romans who had lost all faith in the old religion were by temperament little attracted to the 'gay religions full of pomp and gold', in Milton's words, which the East offered. Instead they turned to find solace in the last gift that Hellas had to bestow, Greek philosophy.

Below. Neptune, assimilated to Poseidon. The trident was the weapon favoured by tunny-fishers, the most important Mediterranean fishery. The whip in his right hand reminds us that Poseidon was also a controller of horses. This statue came from Anzio. Musei Vaticani.

Epicureans and Stoics

The interpolation of a chapter on philosophy in a book purporting to deal with religion may seem like an attempt to mislead. It very easily could be, because religion and philosophy are, generally speaking, two different things. But there are two reasons for making an exception in the present case. The first is that Greek philosophy, particularly one school of it, did have a profound influence not only on Roman minds but on Roman morals as well; the second is that this same school proclaimed an ethic which Christianity in large measure assimilated, so that it is to this day part of Roman religious tradition.

Athenian Philosophy

We are apt to associate Greek philosophy primarily with Athens, and rightly, for by the time of which we are treating, namely the third century B.C., Athens had become the centre of the philosophic world. The first Greek philosophers arose however not in Athens nor even on the Greek mainland but in Asia Minor, in Ionia or the islands adjacent to it. They were among the great pioneers of human thought, because they were the first to seek a rational explanation of the universe. As early as the seventh century B.C. these men discarded the myths about gods and goddesses, even though so many of the tales had been consecrated by Homer, himself an Ionian. The Ionian seekers were looking for something more definable, if not more definite, as a first cause. Very often they were materialists, which is what makes them so startlingly modern. Surely, they argued, there must be a First Cause, a basic element? One proposed fire, another water, another eternal flux. Unfortunately we possess almost nothing of the writings of these philosophers, except a number of 'sayings' of Heracleitus – not very illuminating, really: he was known even to his contemporaries as 'the dark'. The importance of these early enquirers lies less in the solutions they proposed to the everlasting question than in their being the first to put that question. Then came two new proposals, which were to have a great and abiding influence. Democritus of Abdera (which is in eastern Macedonia, but Democritus belongs to the Ionian School) put forward his atomic theory. He suggested that all matter is composed of *atoma*, that is of particles which cannot be cut or divided. Democritus' theory was, be it noted, purely speculative, like most Greek theories. They were seldom followed up by experiment, because few Greeks were interested in practical applications. Only in medicine and astronomy did Greeks, of the Hellenistic age, make 'practical' experiments, and in these two arts, specially astronomy, they made amazing progress. Democritus' theory is nevertheless of great importance, because it influenced Epicurus, and through him one of the greatest poets of all time, Lucretius.

The purveyors of 'mind' if they may so be called are important for a different reason: it was they who had the greatest impact on Athens at the height of its power and glory in the age of Pericles. Indeed so taken was Pericles with the new philosophy of dominant Mind, and with its exponents, specially his pet philosopher, Anaxagoras of Miletus, that the Athenians nicknamed him Mind, *nous*.

This idea of Mind became paramount in Athens. It influenced Plato and later philosophers including the Stoics.

We learn from *Acts* that when Saint Paul visited Athens in A.D. 59 it was with the Epicureans and Stoics that he disputed. They had established themselves as the chief schools long before, and it was these two that were to influence Rome. Let us now briefly examine their doctrines.

The conquests of Alexander mark one of the indisputable turning-points of history. The whole basis on which the polity and thought of Athens and of many another Greek society had been organised, namely the city state, had been abolished for ever and replaced by a multiracial society organised in massive units which overstepped national boundaries. The political and ethical works of Aristotle, who had been Alexander's tutor, were obsolete almost as soon as he had written them. For Aristotle, as for Plato, it was axiomatic that the 'good life', that is happiness in its highest sense, was possible only to those who played an active part in the service of society — which took the form of the little self-contained state, or *polis*. But that had now been swept away, just as in our own day the little, rounded society of parish or borough has been swept away by agglomerations controlled by wholly different lines of interest. And just as in our day people are looking for new sanctions for new modes of conduct, so in the post-Alexandrine age they made the same quest.

It was philosophy which provided the answer. No longer were philosophers interested in metaphysical abstractions, that is they were no longer primarily intellectual innovators, they sought to furnish ethical guidance. For Cicero, writing in the first century B.C. but reflecting the teaching of the third, philosophy is the 'art or guide of life', 'the training or healing of the soul'. Plutarch in the next century called it 'the only medicine for spiritual diseases'. The state of affairs is perfectly summed up by C. F. Angus writing in the *Cambridge Ancient History* (VII, 231): 'Metaphysics sink into the background, and ethics, now individual, become of the first importance. Philosophy is no longer the pillar of fire going before a few intrepid seekers after truth; it is rather an ambulance following in the wake of the struggle for existence and picking up the weak and wounded.'

In meeting this human, individual need, two schools above all others succeeded, the Epicureans and the Stoics.

Epicurus

Epicurus was born in 341 B.C., of Athenian parentage, and lived in Samos with his father until the age of twenty-one when the Athenian settlers in the island were expelled by one of Alexander's generals. After fifteen years spent as a displaced person, a refugee, he came to Athens and established himself and his school in a garden on the outskirts of the city. Here he taught, in happy seclusion, for the rest of his days, dying in 270. He had a genius for friendship, and his pupils, who included slaves and women, were devoted to him.

Epicurus's system was based on the atomic theory of Democritus, although Epicurus himself never acknowledged his debt to his predecessor. This theory maintained that all matter consists of streams of atoms which flow in parallel channels, only that occasionally some atoms swerve, and so produce new combinations, including our universe. The doctrine of the swerve is variously explained. Cicero suggests that Epicurus was suddenly struck by the brilliant idea that unless an atom did swerve now and then, nothing would be created at all — the atoms would just go on pouring through space without ever colliding or cohering. The orthodox explanation however seems to have been that the theory is a direct deduction from experience: we know that there is a universe and therefore the atoms must have collided to create it. As a corollary, we know that we have free will, and this too, like everything else, must be the product of atoms. So the atoms swerve, and experience does not disprove this, because no-one can show that they do not.

Thus evolution is a purely natural, material process, with which gods have nothing to do. Gods there may be, but they are remote beings, utterly unconcerned with man. It follows that any concept of hell, or of divine punishment is folly. There is no heaven, either, beyond the grave. 'Therefore Death, the king of terrors, is nothing to us, because as long as we exist Death is not present, and when Death is come we are no more.'

Superstition — that is the great enemy. But there is a worse one, and this observation is of particular interest to twentieth-century students. In one of his letters, quoted by a later writer, Epicurus says: 'It were better to follow the fairy-tales of gods than to be a slave to the determinism of the scientists. The one does suggest a hope of appeasing the gods by reverencing them, but the other implies a Necessity which is implacable.'

It was a philosophy of escape, of quietism – just how quiet may be judged by the fact that from the death of Epicurus until the final disappearance of the school six centuries later no change in its teaching is recorded. It was static, embalmed. The true Epicurean would concentrate on achieving *ataraxía* peace and quiet, untroubled tranquillity. He would avoid public life (what a reversal of the attitude of Plato and Aristotle!), passion or even matrimony.

Noble natures might find in this philosophy a guide to the contemplative life; but for the more vulgar majority it seemed to offer a rational basis for a life of self-indulgence. It was all the more unfortunate therefore that Epicureanism should have reached Rome just when materialism and sensual excess were making such inroads among the young. The Romans when they took up Epicurus's philosophy tended to degrade and pervert it, and so to give to the word 'epicure' the sense we now attach to it. But two of Rome's greatest poets were followers of this brave and lovable man, one being the gentlest and most amiable of them all, Horace; the other, Lucretius whose atomic epic *On the Nature of Things* is the greatest poem of its kind in any language. It helped to inspire Virgil, and is reflected in many of our own poets, including Gray and Tennyson. Of no other Greek philosopher can this be said.

Zeno

Far different was the origin and influence of Epicurus's contemporary Zeno, founder of the Stoics. Zeno was not a Greek. He was the son of a Phoenician merchant of Kitium in Cyprus. He was very ugly, had a feeble constitution and was rather dark, so that people called him 'the Egyptian'. He reached Athens in the year 314 B.C. as a shipwrecked pauper. His vessel had gone down with all its cargo and Zeno was ruined. He walked up from Piraeus to Athens, where he dolefully entered a bookseller's shop and started browsing, to take his mind off his troubles. The book he had picked up happened to be Xenophon's *Memoirs of Sokrates*. Zeno was charmed with them – more: he decided then and there to take up philosophy himself. 'Who is your leading philosopher nowadays?' he asked the bookseller. 'Krates – he's just gone by' was the reply. Out dashed Zeno, caught up with Krates and asked to become his disciple. Krates agreed to give him a trial and after putting him through some humiliating preliminary tests admitted him as a pupil. For thirteen years Zeno sat at the feet of Krates and other philosophers and then in 301 he commenced as a teacher himself. Having no money to hire a hall, he taught in the famous painted Porch or Stoa, where Polygnotus had represented the defeat of the Persians, at the northern end of the Agora. Hence his disciples were called Stoics. Like Epicurus, Zeno was greatly beloved, so much so that the Athenians (among other honours) entrusted to him the keys of the city.

As already noted Zeno was a Semite; and the mark of all Semetic doctrine from Isaiah to Muhammad is an uncompromising belief in eternal order, combined with an intolerance of the imperfect amounting to a sense of sin. In the eyes of a Stoic there was nothing fortuitous about the universe: it was governed, and governed by an immutable law which it was wicked to transgress. It was primarily this insistence on the rule of law that commended Stoicism to the disciplined Roman mind. The wise man is he who can tell evil from good and walk accordingly. For their physics the Stoics went back to Heracleitus, and postulated fire as the ultimate reality. Fire is also Reason or God. Zeno's originality showed itself in identifying the intellectual *logos* or reason of the Socratics, that is to say the principle which regulates human thinking and action, with the material *logos* of Heracleitus. Thus, the reason which rules the cosmos is the same as the reason which dwells in our hearts and rules our lives. Therefore the Law

of the Universe is also the law of our own natures and we can only realise ourselves by conforming to the divine purpose, whose service is perfect freedom. This idea is wholly Semitic, and quite unGreek; to a Greek *man* was the measure of all things, and *aspiration* was alien to him.

This concept led to a cosmopolitan view of humanity, based on logic. Seneca the great Roman exponent of Stoicism in the first century A.D., would write: 'Each of us has two fatherlands, one the country in which we happen to be born, the other an empire upon which the sun never sets.' The Epicureans denied providence: for the Stoics it was the ruler of the world.

Curiously enough, as two modern English scholars have noted, the best expositor of the religious and metaphysical aspect of Stoicism is to be found in the Roman Catholic poet Alexander Pope – or perhaps not so curiously: as already noted much of Stoicism was carried over into Christianity, and Pope, is here, in his *Essay on Man*, reflecting the fashionable Deism of the eighteenth century which had sprung from it.

All are but parts of one stupendous
*   whole,*
Whose body Nature is, and God the
*   soul;*
That changed through all, and yet in
*   all the same,*
Great in the earth, as in the etherial
*   frame,*
Warms in the sun, refreshes in the
*   breeze,*
Glows in the stars, and blossoms in
*   the trees,*
Lives through all life, extends
*   through all extent,*
Spreads undivided, operates unspent,
Breathes in our soul, informs our
*   mortal part,*
As full, as perfect, in a hair as heart;
As full, as perfect, in vile man that
*   mourns,*
As the rapt seraph that adores and
*   burns:*
To him no high, no low, no great,
*   no small,*
He fills, he bounds, connects and
*   equals all.*

Cease then, nor order imperfection
*   name;*
Our proper bliss depends on what
*   we blame.*
Know thy own point: this kind, this
*   due degree*
Of blindness, weakness, Heaven
*   bestows on thee,*
Submit; in this or any other sphere,
Secure to be as blest as thou canst
*   bear;*
Safe in the natal, or the mortal
*   hour.*
All nature is but art, unknown to
*   thee;*
All chance, direction which thou
*   canst not see;*
All discord, harmony not
*   understood;*
All partial evil universal good;
And spite of pride, in erring reason's
*   spite,*
One truth is clear – Whatever is, is
*   right.*

Panaetius

It was Rome's good fortune that its first knowledge of Stoicism was conveyed to it by an outstanding Greek. Panaetius was a persuasive and upright man, and by birth a Rhodian, that is a citizen of a Greek state with which Rome, despite her increasing imperialism at the expense of the Hellenes, had always been on good terms. Panaetius was a convinced and eloquent Stoic, and it is not surprising that when he visited Rome, he should be drawn into the charmed and charming circle of the Scipios. Publius Cornelius Scipio Aemilianus, who was born in 184, was a man of real elevation of mind. The son of the famous Aemilius Paulus, the conqueror of Perseus of Macedon, he had been adopted into the family of the Scipios, and so had won the friendship of Polybius, a Greek diplomatist and historian who was already a member of the distinguished household. Polybius treated the boy as his son, and young Scipio (as he now was) regarded the genial historian as his father. They were lifelong friends and their social circle included the élite of Rome during its hey-day.

In this already philhellene family, who spoke Greek, wrote Greek, and

had so many personal connections with Greece, it was natural that Panaetius should find a welcome, and that like Polybius he should become a resident friend of Scipio himself. 'From Panaetius, Scipio and his friends would learn', in Warde-Fowler's phrase, 'a new and illuminating conception of man's place in the universe, and of his relation to the Power manifested in it.' This was an unprecedented enlargement of Roman religious consciousness.

At the same time, Panaetius realised that the pure Stoicism in which he had been brought up must be modified for Roman consumption. For one thing, whereas Zeno had taught at a time when the Greek city state was disappearing, Rome still was a city state, and was rapidly becoming an imperial power. Politics and political theory must therefore still be an essential element in any system designed to be a guide for Romans. Secondly, the Romans were practical people, little attracted to speculation in any form. Emphasis must therefore be laid on the duties of the ordinary citizen, and the necessity of living in accordance with nature.

Panaetius made the requisite concessions and adjustments, and so his system found favour in Roman minds. Cicero in many of his philosophical writings reproduces Panaetius' Romanised Stoicism.

This was a great victory for Greek thought. Rome had not taken kindly to the first philosophers she had met. In 173 B.C. two Epicurean philosophers had been expelled from the city: eighteen years later certain eminent Athenian philosophers who had come to Rome on a diplomatic mission, as soon as they started to expound their ideas, were asked to leave. All the more fortunate therefore the conjunction of Panaetius, Polybius and Scipio: at least a beacon had been lit.

Stoicism is a chilly creed; it could never console a Horace or inspire a Lucretius, but in the first century A.D. it would be the guide of Seneca, and in the second produce two of its most famous exponents, one a slave,

Epictetus, the other an emperor, Marcus Aurelius. Stoicism cleared the way for a universal religion, and Saint Paul could quote a Stoic hymn in proclaiming that religion. What Stoicism lacked was what all puritan creeds lack, a really active enthusiasm for human beings as such. Most philosophies lack that. The most cursory survey of the history of philosophies shows how transitory most of them have proved. Philosophy is a battery, whereas religion is a dynamo. Stoicism was bound by the limitations inherent in its nature; but it was a big step forward.

A funerary urn in the Syracuse National Museum. The eagle on the lid symbolises the hope that the deceased will mount to the skies. Museo Archeologico Nazionale, Syracuse.

Immortal Longings

Despite its inherent limitations, philosophy was to beget the first comprehension of the sublime to irradiate Rome. In this study, as in so much else connected with Roman religion, we must not allow ourselves to be dazed by hindsight, that is, we must not compare the achievements of republican Rome in the spiritual realm with that of the Rome of apostles, martyrs and saints. We must try, rather, to view the Rome of the first century B.C. from a strictly 'B.C.' stance. If we succeed in so doing we shall be surprised and heartened by the prospect we survey — and we shall be all the more depressed by the waves of eastern exoticism which were to follow it.

In order to establish the right perspective for what we are about to examine, let us once more regard the traditional, official religion as it appeared in the last days of the Republic. It is best described by Jérome Carcopino in his now classic *Daily Life in Ancient Rome*. Carcopino is writing of the second century A.D., but his analysis applies equally to an earlier period, so rigid did Rome's *jus divinum* become so early:

'The Roman pantheon still persisted, apparently immutable; and the ceremonies which had for centuries been performed on the dates prescribed by the pontiffs from their sacred calendars continued to be carried out in accordance with ancestral custom. But the spirits of men had fled from the old religion; it still commanded their service but no longer their hearts or their belief. With its indeterminate gods and colourless myths, mere fables concocted from details suggested by Latin topography or pale reflections of the adventures which had overtaken the Olympians of Greek epic; with its prayers formulated in the style of legal contracts and as dry as the procedure of a lawsuit; with its lack of metaphysical curiosity and indifference to moral values; with the narrow-minded banality of its field of action, limited to the interests of the city and the development of practical politics — Roman religion froze the impulses of faith by its coldness and its prosaic utilitarianism. It sufficed at most to reassure a soldier against the risks of war or a peasant against the rigours of unseasonable weather, but . . . it had wholly lost its power over the hearts of men.'

Cicero

Against this background the mysticism of Cicero and his like appears all the more original, all the more noble. Cicero's reputation suffered violent ups and downs during his own lifetime, and it has been, as it were, a barometer for determining the moral and political atmosphere of succeeding ages. Cicero has been lauded as the greatest of Romans, he has been despised as the meanest of statesmen. Because he wrote so much, and so incomparably beautifully, and because we possess even today so many of his letters, Cicero is known to us more intimately than any other Roman. And that means that we know his faults as well as his excellences. Unfortunately his two most glaring defects were two that Anglo-Saxons particularly dislike — vanity and timidity, both of which in Cicero reached pathological proportions. But his virtues were outstanding. Not only did he create Latin as we know it, as Dante was to create Italian, but

A mosaic of Neptune
Triumphant with his
consort, Amphitrite,
and surrounded by
his subjects. Musée
du Louvre, Paris

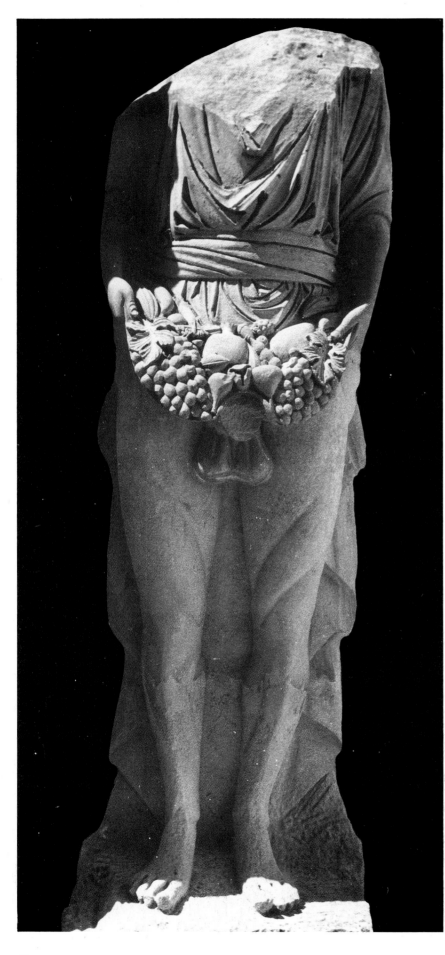

Cicero's spiritual outlook was as lofty as that of any Roman of whom we have record. Before Rome goes down under the oriental flood it is well to follow Cicero to the heights. Cicero was an eclectic. With Epicureanism he had no sympathy. He was attracted by the morality of the Stoics, but accounted himself an Academic.

Pythagoras

The source of his transcendental view of the world was not Stoicism. It was, rather, the teachings of Pythagoras, who, like Heracleitus, was one of the great Ionians, having been born in the island of Samos. In about 530 B.C. he migrated to Croton, a Greek settlement in the south of Italy. Pythagoras is known to many as a great mathematician and astronomer, but his philosophy had a religious side to it as well. At Croton he organised a brotherhood bound by strict rules. His most important doctrine was the transmigration of souls, an idea borrowed from an older cult of Orpheus. The belief in a future life, the conception of this life as only a preparation for another, and the need for purgation by asceticism, these are truly religious doctrines. Pythagoras was expelled from Croton on political grounds and his teaching proscribed; but it must have always lain dormant among the Greek colonies of southern Italy. 'He held Magna Graecia', says Cicero of Pythagoras, 'as much by his

Left. Statue of Priapus, god of fertility. Generally shown as a misshapen old man, he was adopted as a god of gardens, where his statue was often erected. This statue shows him supporting kindly fruits of the earth. Musée du Bardo, Algiers.

Opposite. The eagle, a favourite motif in Roman monumental stone work.

authority as by the prestige of his teaching; and many centuries later so flourishing was the fame of the Pythagoreans that no others seemed to be learned men.' Plato himself is believed to have journeyed to southern Italy to study this philosophy and to learn the principle of the immortality of the soul. How it reached Rome we do not know. There was a fantastic plot in 181, after the Hannibalic war, when some impostors pretended to have found Numa's coffin on the Janiculan Hill, and inside it not Numa's body but a stone coffer containing alleged writings by Numa about Pythagorean teaching. These came into the hands of a praetor who with the approval of the Senate publicly burnt the forged books.

The war had brought Rome into contact with southern Italy, but we hear no more of the doctrine, so subversive of Rome's traditional religion, for a century, after which lapse of time a number of Pythagorean documents began to circulate, but with what effect we have no inkling. The man who really made Pythagoreanism 'stick' in Rome was Posidonius, a traveller, philosopher and historian who dominated the intellectual scene in Rome during the first half of the first century B.C. His writings, of which we possess a few fragments only, 'lie at the back', in Warde Fowler's words, 'of nearly all the serious Roman literature of his own and in-deed of the following age.' Panaetius, there can be little doubt, had done something to leaven Stoicism with Platonic-Aristotelian psychology, the general tendency of which was towards a dualism of soul and body.

The pure Stoics admitted no distinction or difference between heaven and earth, soul and body – they were pantheists – nor could they admit the idea of a transcendent God. Their passion for unity inhibited them. But once Panaetius had heralded a return to an older mode of thought, it was easy for a society which had long ago abandoned burial for cremation and had given up any idea of the prolongation of human life beneath the earth to follow his lead. Posidonius pursued this line of thought, and so 'at once gave to mysticism – or transcendentalism if we choose so to call it – its chance. For in such a dualistic psychology it is the soul that gains and the body that loses.'

This was the faith which Cicero has illustrated so beautifully and sensitively. His eulogy of the Pythagoreans has already been quoted: it occurs in his *Tusculan Disputations*, written in 64 B.C., the year before he became Consul. Ten years later Cicero started work on a *Republic*, in imitation of Plato's, a topic he had long been contemplating. The book came out three years later and at once became popular. Cicero imagines that Scipio Africanus Minor, mentioned in the last chapter, has assembled a company of friends, in the year 129 B.C., in the garden of his home, where they discuss forms of government, man's place in the state, and the duties of a statesman. As Cicero explained to his brother he had set the discussion in a past age for fear of causing offence – he was living in dangerous days. The work owes much to Plato, to his *Republic* first and foremost; and the idea of placing the scene in the last year of the chief speaker's life may have come from the *Phaedo*, as also that of concluding the book with a passage which concentrates on life after death. In much of the argument we can trace the influence of Posidonius, and Cicero makes Scipio say that he had often discussed the subject of the state with Panaetius in the presence of Polybius, whose ideas it also reflects. The most famous part of the work is its conclusion. Scipio relates that when he was serving in Africa as a regimental officer in 149, at the beginning of the Third Punic War, in which he was to win renown, he one night dreamed a dream, in which his famous grandfather appeared to him and after foretelling his future career warns him of life's dangers too. (In fact, as all Cicero's readers knew, the younger Scipio was found dead in his bed one day in 129 B.C., the supposed year of the *Republic*'s setting. He was buried hugger-mugger and the cause of death was never established.) 'But',

the elder Scipio goes on, 'be assured of this, Africanus, so that you may be the more eager to defend the commonwealth: all those who have preserved, or aided or enlarged their fatherland have a special place reserved for them in the heavens where they may enjoy an eternal life – *aevo sempiterno* – of happiness. For nothing of all that is done on earth is more pleasing to the supreme God who rules the whole universe – *illi principi deo qui omnem mundum regit* – than the assemblies and gatherings of men associated in justice which are called states. Their rulers and preservers come from that place and to that place they return.' Scipio then asks his grandfather whether his father Paulus and the others whom we think of as dead are really alive. 'Surely', he replies, 'all those are alive who have escaped from the bondage of the body as from a prison; but that life of yours which men so call is really death.' Paulus then approaches. Scipio the younger is much overcome by his apparition, and asks why he should remain on earth: could he not hasten to his father? No, replies his father, unless that God 'whose temple is everything that you see has freed

Above. Three Etruscan musicians on a tomb fresco in Tarquinia. Tomb of the Leopards.

you from the prison of the body, you cannot gain entrance hither.' Bidding him love justice and duty he says: 'Such a life is the road to the skies, to that gathering of those who have completed their earthly lives and have been relieved of the body and who live in yonder place you now see . . . and which you on earth, borrowing a Greek term, call the Galaxy.'

The younger Scipio is enraptured by what he sees in this high heaven to which he has been borne, enraptured too by the music of the spheres. How small earth looks: even the Roman empire (and he uses thus early the word *imperium*) seems but a speck. His grandfather bids him, 'Strive on, indeed, and be sure that it is not you who are mortal, but only this body . . . the spirit is your true self, not that physical figure. Know then that you are a god, if a god is that which lives, feels, remembers and foresees and which rules the body over which it is set just as the supreme God above us moves the universe. Finally he conjures his grandson to remember that the great First Cause is a spirit; 'the only force which moves itself, it surely has no beginning and is immortal'. 'He departed, and I awoke from sleep.' So ends Cicero's *Republic*.

Here we have Cicero, one of the greatest Romans of his day, indeed of all time, clearly caught up in the current of mysticism which was then in vogue. But, as Warde Fowler points out, even more significant for the purposes of the present enquiry is Cicero's own behaviour in a personal crisis. In the year 45 B.C. he lost his only daughter Tullia, to whom he had been wholly devoted. She was the light of his life, which was as unhappy domestically as it was troubled politically. In his utter sorrow he writes from one of his country retreats to his friend and confidant Atticus in Rome on 3 May 45 to say he wants not a mere tomb for Tullia, but a shrine. He thought of her as being still living. 'I want it to be a shrine – *fanum* – and that wish cannot be rooted out of my heart. I am anxious to avoid any likeness to a tomb, not so much on account of the penalty of the law,

Above. A mosaic showing the head of a young Satyr. Museo Nazionale Romano, Rome.

Right. Detail of a mosaic pavement from Genazzano which shows the god Pan. Museo Nazionale Romano, Rome.

[which forbade intramural burial] as in order to attain as nearly as possible to an *apotheosis* [he uses the Greek word]. This I could do if I built it in the Villa itself, but, as I have often said, I dread the change of owners. Wherever I construct it on the land, I think that I could secure that posterity should respect its sanctity. I should not like it to be known by any other name than *fanum* – unreasonably you may say.'

Shades of the Underworld

Cicero refers to the project in several later letters. Clearly, he thinks of his beloved child as being still living; he cannot bear to think of her as having passed into the chill, crepuscular company of the *Manes*, as the Romans called the dead. Gradually, it is true, these shades become more individual, until by Cicero's time we begin to come upon those inscriptions, which were to become so common in later centuries, to *Dis Manibus*, the gods of the underworld. The *Manes* were the object of a cult. Wine, honey, milk and flowers were offered to them. Two festivals were devoted to them, the *Rosaria* or *Violaria* when the tombs were strewn with roses or violets, and the *Parentalia*, which lasted from 18 to 21 February. Aeneas was held to have founded the *Parentalia*, in honour of his old father Anchises. One year, it was said, the ghosts invaded the city (no burials were allowed within the walls) and could only be induced to go home to their graves by the due performance of the appropriate rites. When the dead were thought of in this guise, that is not as ancestors quietly resting in their graves but as evil spirits on the rampage, they were called *Lemures*, and they were dealt with at the *Lemuria*, celebrated on 9, 11 and 13 May. The ceremony to remove these malevolent ghosts from the city was carried out at night.

Traditionalism in Religion

The paterfamilias walked out of the house barefoot, washed his hands in spring-water, and then turning his head away, threw out into the night handfulls of beans, crying out: 'By these beans I redeem me and mine'. This he said nine times without looking round, while the Lemurs, it was said, gathered up the beans. After that the celebrant washed his hands once more, beat on a bronze vessel and said: 'Shades of my ancestors begone'. He might then look round, and, behold, they were gone.

Cicero was probably not the only Roman of his day who regarded this sort of thing as a Hallowe'en charade; but how very much further Cicero had gone towards a more sublime and spiritual view of human destiny! In official life he was a strict upholder of traditional religion. He wrote a sequel to his *Republic* called *Laws*, in which he sets out the laws by which his ideal state is to be governed. In the second book of this work he deals with religion. No-one, he enjoins, is to have private gods, either new gods or alien gods unless recognised by the state. In private men are to worship their ancestral gods. In cities they are to have shrines, in the country, groves and homes for the *Lares*. The gods to be worshipped are to be not only those which have always been regarded as dwellers in heaven, but also those whose merits have admitted them to heaven: Hercules, Liber (that is, Bacchus or Dionysus), Aesculapius, Castor, Pollux, Quirinus; also good qualities such as Intellect, Virtue, Loyalty and Good Faith.

Gods are to have their own priests, who are to see that all is done decently and in order. The Vestal Virgins shall guard the sacred fire on the public hearth. Those who are ignorant of the prescribed rites shall seek information of the priests. Soothsayers, augurs and other such persons recognised by the state shall interpret omens and portents. The Senate may refer such phenomena to Etruscan soothsayers. Women must not perform sacrifices by night except those for the *Bona Dea*, from which men are excluded; and the initiation into the Roman form of the Eleusinian mysteries is to be properly safeguarded. No-one shall make collections on behalf of Cybele except her own servants, and then they may do

so only on specified days.

What a seeming contradiction is here, between Cicero the transcendental mystic and Cicero the traditionalist. In Roman minds no such contradiction need exist. To maintain the *mos maiorum*, the ancestral custom, was an act of piety. In a society which lacked modern means of com-

munication, the beliefs and attitudes of the ruling class had an influence which they would not exert today, except in tribal communities, where a tribesman on being asked what his attitude is to an issue may answer in a voice of surprise, 'How can I say until I have asked my Chief?' For Cicero, therefore, as for Varro, *pietas*

was a matter of practice, not of belief. And during the disturbed years of the first century B.C. practice had fallen into sad disarray. As Cicero himself laments, auspices were cynically misused for political ends; prodigies, as Livy tells us, were not recorded or never announced; the calendar as we have seen fell into hopeless chaos,

A detail from the so-called 'Nozze Aldobrandine' showing women taking part in wedding rites. This famous fresco is in the Musei Vaticani.

temples were allowed to fall into ruin, even the great shrine of Jupiter on the Capitol which, burnt in 83, was not fully restored for 21 years. The office of Flamen Dialis was not filled from Sulla's dictatorship, that is from some time between 81 and 79, until 11 B.C. – though in view of the antique taboos with which he was hedged that was perhaps not surprising. Pietas, therefore, must be maintained and stimulated by every possible means.

That is the first point which emerges from a study of Cicero's beliefs. It is of the utmost importance for the comprehension of the religious history of Rome during the next four centuries. Exactly the same arguments in favour of the upholding of traditional cults and rites would be used by refined and intelligent pagans of the fourth century A.D. in their disputes, often by then quite amicable, with Christians. The second point to be grasped is no less important and significant: it is the current conception of divinity.

Deification

In his own commentary on these laws contained in a later chapter of the same book, Cicero says, touching the deification of heroes, 'Now the law which prescribes the worship of those of the human race who have been deified – *consecratos* – such as Hercules and the rest, makes it clear that while the souls of all men are immortal, those of good and brave men are divine. It is a good thing also that Intellect, Loyalty, Virtue and Good Faith should be deified by a stroke of the pen – *manu* – and in Rome temples have been dedicated by the state to all these qualities, the purpose being that those who possess them (and all good men do) should believe that the gods themselves are established in their own souls.'

This view of divinity is diametrically opposed to that of the Jews and the Christians. For the Jews, God is supreme, eternal, alone and incomprehensibly elevated. He may communicate with men, but he remains alone and one. For the Christians, this one God had been pleased to become man, while still remaining God, and in that human guise to visit humanity. What could be more different than a man becoming a god at the behest of man, and a God becoming man of his own will? Nothing.

That is why the struggle between the state religion of Rome in which the godhead of the ruler was progressively enhanced and the Christians to whom the mere idea was blasphemy was to be so harsh and prolonged.

Before we come to deal with that struggle it will be appropriate to return to the other Eastern religions which were to precede its advent; and in so doing to salute Cicero once again as being so far in advance of others of his day and generation.

Orontes Nile and Tiber

In one of the most famous sneers ever uttered the Roman satirist Juvenal, writing at the beginning of the empire's second century, complains that 'Long ago the Orontes emptied itself into the Tiber', meaning that all the pollutions of the Levant had become acclimatised in Rome. Juvenal was a humourless pessimist who thought that every question had two sides, both bad. In his day, it is true, the word 'oriental' had acquired something of the pejorative sense that attaches to the word 'Levantine' in our own age; but it is essential to remember that in Juvenal's day and for several centuries before and after him, the east was far more fertile in ideas, in the arts, in philosophy, in learning and in religion than the west. The extent of the intellectual vacuum of the west can be gauged from one very simple fact, that in the great land-mass now occupied by Spain, Portugal and France, the Latin language at once supplanted the local dialects (so that those countries still use a 'latin' tongue) because only in Latin could anyone, native or Roman, exchange any thought which required precise expression. In the east, on the other hand, Latin never supplanted either the vernacular Aramaic or Egyptian, still less the Greek which since the days of Alexander had been the international language. Latin (as we know, for instance, from the inscription on the cross of Jesus of Nazareth) became simply a third, official tongue.

The east gave Rome far more than Rome gave the east. In discussing the influx of eastern religions, as we are about to do, it is well to bear this in mind. Some of these oriental cults were by no means elevated, and those appealed to the mob; but others were of a far higher standard. The general attraction of these religions is thus put by Cumont:

'The oriental religions, by appealing at one and the same time to the senses, the reason and the conscience, gripped the entire personality. They seemed to offer, by comparison with those of the past, more beauty in their ceremonies, more truth in their teaching, a higher standard in their moral outlook. The splendid rites of their festivals, their devotions, now grand, now moving, sad or triumphant, captivated the mass of the simple and lowly. The progressive revelation of an antique wisdom, inherited from the old and distant orient, won the minds of the educated. The emotions which these religions stimulated, the consolations which they offered, chiefly attracted women: it was in them that the priests of Isis and Cybele found their most ardent and most generous adherents, their most enthusiastic propagandists. Mithras, on the other hand, gathered round him only men, on whom he imposed a rough sort of moral discipline. Every soul, in short, was vanquished by the promise of spiritual purification, and the infinite vista of eternal bliss.'

Egyptian Religion

Cybele has already been mentioned, Isis, although she never attained the official status of the Great Mother, became an extremely popular deity throughout the Roman world. Her august and mysterious origin was no doubt in part responsible for her vogue. Egypt, although it fronts the Mediterranean, is not a Mediterranean country. All around the midland sea, save only in Egypt, the terrain

and the climate are astonishingly uniform. The limestone hills, clad with olive, pomegranate and myrtle, the cornfields and the vineyards – these are to be found in Turkey as they are in Spain, in Palestine, as in Greece or Algeria. The Greek colonist found himself at home in the Hellespont or in Magna Graecia: the Syrian trader established his factories in Delos or Tangier. Only Egypt is alien to this familiar world. Here there are no hills nor trees. The land lives not from its own resources, refreshed by the rain from heaven, but is nurtured from without by a magical and life-giving stream, whose very origins were unknown until the nineteenth century. Nowhere is the contrast between life and death more vivid than in Egypt, where it is possible quite literally to stand with one foot in the desert and the other in the sown. From a remote antiquity, from an age far anterior to the first kings of Hellas or Crete, the Egyptians had pondered the great mystery of life and death, and had raised what are still the grandest and most imposing funerary monuments in the world. Persia, Greece and Rome were all in their turn fascinated by Egypt. The father of Greek history, Herodotus, in the fifth century B.C. devoted a whole book of his great work to Egypt. Alexander the Great founded there his greatest creation, Alexandria; and his successors, the Ptolemies, while preserving the ancient heritage of the Pharoahs, made of Alexandria one of the most active cultural centres of the Greek world. After the defeat of Antony and Cleopatra, Egypt became the appanage of the Caesars, who embellished their own capital with Egyptian obelisks, just as London, Paris and New York would one day be proud to do.

Egyptian deities were bound to find their way to Rome. That they did so when they did and to the extent they did is due to the sagacity of the first Ptolemy. He realised that many of the traditional Egyptian gods, in animal shape, hawks or dogs, jackals or crocodiles would never be received by Greeks with anything but ridicule (Juvenal sneered at them too). He therefore hit on the idea of making Isis and her mate Osiris the centre of a new devotion, subtly hellenising the resulting deity. He was called Serapis,

Opposite. Probably the best example of a bust of Serapis. This one was discovered during recent excavations in the City. Museum of London.

Below. Cybele and Attis. These were two of the most popular importations from the Orient. Here they are depicted on an altar A.D. 295, Roman, but of Near Eastern origin.

from Usur-Api, or Osiris-Apis, originally the god who protected the necropolis of Memphis. Alexandria, the new capital, was to be the metropolis of the new religion. Greek was to be its liturgical language. The cult-statue was a magnificent creation by an Athenian sculptor, Bryaxis, a contemporary of Scopas. Thus hellenised, brought to the coast from the interior, and embodied in an Athenian image, the new religion set forth conquering and to conquer. The original Serapeum was the model for many others: by the second century A.D. there were

forty-two in Egypt alone.

Isis was not only the wife of Osiris, she was the mother of Horus the sun-god. Set, the lord of the underworld, killed Osiris, who was avenged by Horus on the morrow (in one version of the myth). During the intervening night, Isis had been searching for the dismembered body of Osiris. She finally found it at Byblos, the ancient Phoenician port on the Syrian coast, and restored her husband to life. From the beginning of the new cult, Osiris and Serapis were identified, and the new deity becomes ruler of the dead, imparting to them a share of his own immortality. Isis is the great mother, the mother of gods and of all nature, victorious over the powers of night. She very early possessed her own mysteries, and that made it all the easier to assimilate her to Greek deities. In fact the identification of Isis with Demeter and of Osiris with Dionysos had been made even before the days of Herodotus. Like Osiris, Dionysos was a god who presided over vegetation and governed the underworld, a god who had been killed by an enemy, torn in pieces and miraculously restored again by a goddess. Isis was also identified with other Greek divinities including Io, who as a result of Zeus's passion and Hera's hatred (the usual pattern) after many adventures, which included swimming across the strait which separates Europe from Asia in the guise of a cow, (whence the name Bos-phorus) ended up in Egypt.

Thus the Greeks could find in Serapis one of their own deities reinforced with all the august prestige of Egyptian worship but without any of its absurdities, or (we must add) obscenities. Indeed, as we learn from Plutarch, the new religion was deliberately balanced from the outset so as to attract both the Egyptians and the Greeks at the same time. A Greek hierophant from Eleusis called Timotheus collaborated with a liberal-minded Egyptian priest from Memphis called Manetho to ensure that it made the widest possible appeal. So well did they succeed that a Greek philosopher, Demetrius of Phaleron, cured of blindness by Serapis, composed hymns in his honour that were still being sung more than three centuries later. An elaborate hymnology soon developed of which transcriptions on papyrus have come down to us.

Thus, says Cumont, 'The Greeks ought to be disposed to welcome a cult in which they found their own divinities and their own myths with something added which was more poignant, more magnificent. It is a remarkable fact that among the multitude of deities honoured in the provinces of the kingdom of the Ptolemies those of the entourage, or one might say the cycle, of Osiris, his spouse Isis, their son Harpocrates and their faithful servant Anubis are the only ones which were truly adopted by Hellenic populations. All the other spirits, celestial or infernal, which Egypt worshipped remained strangers in Greece.' The cult of Serapis was 'the most civilised of all the "barbarian" religions: it preserved enough of the exotic to tickle the curiosity of the Greeks, but not enough to wound their delicate sense of moderation – and its success was brilliant.'

In those days as in later epochs the axiom *cuius regio eius religio* – 'whose is the realm, his is the religion' – prevailed; and so wherever king Ptolemy was obeyed or honoured his gods would be obeyed and honoured, too. The priests of Isis under the empire always mentioned the ruling

Right. Isis was a purely Egyptian deity, but she made a wide appeal in the Graeco-Roman world. She was the wife of Osiris, and the mother of the sun-god Horus. As the bereaved mother, she became assimilated to Demeter, and came to represent for her votaries the universal feminine. This statue shows her holding the *sistrum* associated with her worship. It is still used by Abyssinian Christians. Museo del Palazzo dei Conservatori, Rome.

Opposite. Anubis was an Egyptian god with a dog's head. Even when, as in this statue, he is dressed in Greek garb, he could excite among Greeks only ridicule, or at best good-humoured laughter, like Bottom with his ass's head. Ptolemy realised this, and so inaugurated the cult of Serapis.

sovereign first in their prayers, a custom they had inherited from their predecessors under the Ptolemies and would hand on to the Christians and Muslims. Serapis reached Cyprus, Sicily, Antioch – even Athens, where he had a temple at the foot of the Acropolis. A shrine was consecrated to him in Halicarnassus, Herodotus' birth-place, in 307.

This new synthetic religion reached Rome by way of Sicily and Magna Graecia. A municipal decree mentions a Serapeum at Puteoli (Pozzuoli), the port through which Paul of Tarsus would later introduce his gospel to Italy, in 105 B.C. About the same date a temple of Isis was dedicated at Pompeii, of which the frescoes demonstrate to this day the vigour of this Alexandrine culture. In Rome where it had arrived not later than the age of Sulla, the new religion was not universally popular. For one thing it was frankly emotional and as such offended Roman ideas of *gravitas*, or dignity. For another it hailed from a country with which during the last years of the Republic Rome was nearly always on bad terms, culminating in the fatal association of Mark Antony with Cleopatra. No less than four times in a decade, in 58, 53, 50 and 48, the Senate ordered the demolition of Egyptian shrines and the overthrow of their statues. After the eclipse of Antony and Cleopatra the cult became more potentially subversive than ever. In 28 it was forbidden to erect altars to the Alexandrine divinities within the *pomœrium*, and

Opposite. Serapis, the synthetic deity, part Egyptian part Greek, who became widely popular. This bronze head, showing him assimilated with Helios, the sun, now in the British Museum, comes from Helmingham Hall, Norfolk. British Museum, London.

Right. Antinoüs, the beautiful Bythinian who was Hadrian's favourite, met his death by drowning in the Nile. Hadrian had him deified, thus introducing into Roman sculpture a live motif such as it had not known for some time – that of a real and not merely mythological youth. Centuries later it would emerge again in Michelangelo's David. Museo Archeologico Nazionale, Naples.

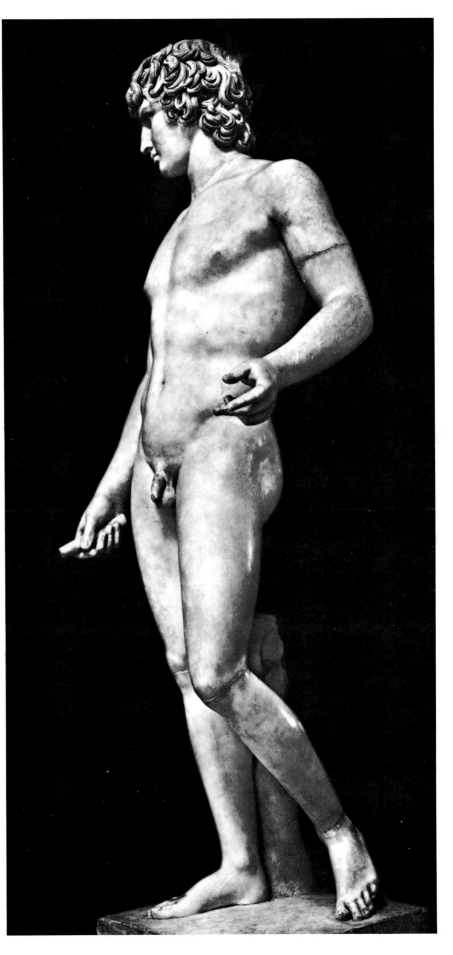

seven years later Agrippa, Augustus' minister, extended the prohibition to a radius of a mile from the city. In A.D. 19, under Tiberius, the Isis-cult provoked a major scandal. A Roman knight called Decius Mundus induced a priest of Isis to persuade a beautiful and gullible dame that if she came to the temple on a certain evening she would be rewarded by intercourse with Anubis. She came, but it was Decius who stood in for the god. This provoked a savage persecution of Isis' votaries.

All to no effect. The religion spread throughout Italy, even while it was proscribed in Rome. Julius Caesar's

reformed calendar had been drawn up by Egyptian savants, who had contribed to slip into it festivals of Isis. With the death of Tiberius the days of repression were over. In the year A.D. 38 Caligula built a grand temple of Isis in the Campus Martius, which Domitian embellished in the most sumptuous style. Future emperors followed suit. The sphinxes and the obelisks multiplied. Hadrian in the second century not only commemorated his favourite Antinoüs by means of an obelisk which still stands in Rome, but included in his Villa at Tibur (Tivoli) a magnificent Serapeum, of which the vestiges still de-

light and impress those who visit it.

Until the very end of the pagan world the worship of Serapis held its ground. In part it was the flexibility, or we might say the vagueness, of its doctrine which made the cult so popular. A sacred scribe, who became one of Nero's preceptors found, in the priestly traditions of his country, echoes of Stoicism. When Plutarch talks of Egyptian deities, he finds that they accord perfectly with his own eclectic views. A Neoplatonist, Iamblichus, finds the same happy concurrence. And not only to Greek goddesses was Isis assimilated: she amalgamated just as easily with the

Phoenician Astarte, the Syrian Atargatis or the Iranian Anahit. She became, in fact, a pantheon in herself; and Serapis is lauded as the One, Zeus, Serapis.

The Egyptian gods, as a Christian apologist attests, had become Roman: the beginning of the third century A.D. saw them at the apogee of their influence. Thereafter they began to yield to Syrian and Persian rivals, and finally to Christianity itself. In the year 394, that is, three years after pagan cults had officially been proscribed, an eyewitness records that their processions still appeared in the streets of Rome; but already

three years earlier Theophilus, patriarch of Alexandria, had burned the great Serapeum to the ground, and had himself initiated the smashing of the famous image. The cult was at an end and yet remarkable vestiges of it survived in Christian practice. Statues of Isis needed hardly more than a change of name to become those of the Virgin Mary. The daily offices, the priestly ablutions, even the tonsure all have their prototypes in Isiac use. To this day, the penitents who ascend the Santa Scala on their knees recall the devotees of Isis who circumambulated her temple in the same posture. The sistrum, the silver rattle

An Isiac procession. The snake was sacred to Isis, which is why Cleopatra, who saw herself as the incarnation of Isis, used it to procure death. The tonsure of the priests of Isis prefigures that of Christian monks. The sistrum is again in evidence.

97

of Isis, still echoes in the Armenian liturgy; and just as the priests of Isis conducted a solemn search for the body of Osiris at Abydos or in Rome, so today the Abyssinians circulate in procession on the roof of the church of the Holy Sepulchre in Jerusalem on Easter Eve, in a symbolic search for the body of Christ.

Syrian Religion

Only one other pagan religion would ever rival the Egyptian deities, before all of them went down before Christianity, and that was the Mithraism of Persia, which in its Roman form became the official religion of the later emperors; but before we come to deal with it, a word or two must be said about the Syrian religions of which the Roman satirist complains.

The religions of Syria never attained in the west the cohesion that those of Egypt, or Asia Minor or Persia did. This is largely due to the nature of the country itself. Syria is divided by high mountain ranges, which run north and south, into many unrelated districts. This has always led not only to political disunity such as it still fosters, but also to a remarkable diversity of religions. Today there are to be found in Syria Muslims, both Sunni and Shia, Jews, Druses, Alaouites and adherents of the Roman Catholic, Orthodox, Syrian, Assyrian, Maronite, Armenian, Greek Catholic, Anglican and Presbyterian churches, to mention only a selection of the larger communions.

The first Syrian goddess to reach Italy was Atargatis, (often confused with the Phoenician Astarte) who had a temple at Bambyce (Membidj) or Hierapolis, not far from the Euphrates. Her worship, which seems to prefigure the antics of the dervishes who still gyrate in Damascus, was in some respects degrading and orgiastic. An old eunuch, of doubtful morals, would precede a troupe of painted youths leading a donkey which bore a decorated image of the goddess. On reaching a village or rich country-house, they would begin their religious exercises. To the sound of highpitched flutes, they started to whirl, with heads thrown back, and

uttering raucous shouts, until they reached a pitch of insensibility, when they would flagellate and slash themselves. The bloodshed delighted the rustic audience, from whom they would take up a handsome collection, added to by a bit of fortune-telling or pocket-picking.

The above picture, based on a novel by Lucius of Patras, is, as Cumont says, no doubt painted too black; but how could any such wandering priests have found their way to Italy? The answer is as slaves. From the third century B.C. onwards, more and more Syrian slaves appeared in Rome. They were highly sought after and men paid more for them than for those of any other race. Syrians were intelligent, biddable and hardy. But their very numbers made them a danger. So, thought the Romans, did the ideas they brought with them; and not only the slaves but the ever growing company of Syrian merchants. In the year 139 B.C. a praetor ordered the expulsion from Rome of Jews and Chaldeans, that is of Syrian soothsayers, for it was they who had brought to Rome the so-called 'science' of astrology. Only five years later a slave revolt, which devastated Sicily, was organised and led by a slave from Apamea, a follower of the Syrian goddess who said he had received his orders from on high. The fact that these wretched beings, too poor to build the simplest shrine, received religious consolation from wandering *Galli*, with whom they shared part of their modest savings, shows how numerous they had become.

A horde of Syrian divinities emigrated all over the empire, and like their Egyptian counterparts they tended to become naturalised. At Puteoli we find Melqart of Sidon as Hercules; Dusares, the god of south Arabia, and Allath, the principal Arab goddess, both moved west via Syria, and Allath became identified with Athena. She even reached Spain, in the company of Hadad of Baalbek-Heliopolis, the relics of whose huge temple still stand on the plain between Beirut and Damascus. The dove and the fish were both wor-

shipped in Syria, the former being sacred to Astarte, the latter, so familiar as an early Christian symbol, to Atargatis.

The most famous of all the Syrian deities was Adonis, whose name is even today a synonym for a rather sloppy type of male beauty. His death was bewailed by Syrian matrons on the shores of the river by Byblos which still runs red with his blood; and he had his 'gardens' in Rome by the time of Augustus.

Among the many Syrian deities which became part of the Western religious heritage none is more strange nor more eloquent of the power of Syria over the humble, than Jupiter of Doliche. Doliche was a small town in Commagene, by the upper Euphrates. Troops from this country served in many parts of the empire, and they took the worship of their protector with them. Not a single literary reference to this god is known, and yet more than a hundred dedications to him have survived, in Africa, Germany, Britain and Hungary among other countries. He was originally a god of lightning, and is represented standing on a bull, and brandishing a thunderbolt in one hand and a hatchet in the other. Being a patron of ironworkers, he was naturally invoked by soldiers for the success of their arms.

These divine migrations were admittedly made for the most part under the empire, but it is convenient to consider them here. They culminated in the elevation of a fourteen-year-old boy, Elagabalus, who was a servitor of the Baal of Emesa (Homs) to the imperial purple, and his introduction into Rome of another 'black stone' as the supreme deity. Because Elagabalus was a foreigner, and because his religious ideas were in advance of his time, he met with hostile treatment from Roman writers. He did in fact attempt to convert Rome to a monotheism based on Sol Invictus, the Unconquered Sun, which half a century later Aurelian succeeded in bringing from Palmyra. Since this monotheism was that in which the first Christian emperor, Constantine, was brought up it has an outstanding claim to notice in any study of Syria's contribution to Rome's religious destiny.

One final contribution of Syria to the religion of Rome may be mentioned, namely the crucifix. During the first five centuries of the Christian era, Christians had a horror of representing their Saviour nailed to an instrument of torture. It was only in the sixth century that the Syrians introduced the symbol in all its pathos.

A priest of Attis. This cult originated in Asia Minor and spread to Rome where, under the Empire, Attis was established as a powerful deity. This bas-relief is from Ostia which, being the sea port of Rome, was naturally a meeting place of many foreign cults. Scave di Ostia.

Moses and Mithras

Before we come to the end of the story, which is the struggle between Caesar and Christ and the ultimate victory of both, there are two more eastern religions to be considered, Judaism and Mithraism. Both exerted a powerful influence on Roman religion and both proclaimed ethical standards superior to any of the other imported cults or to the old Roman religion itself. Both of them, too, owed a great deal to the same source – Persia.

Influences of Judaism

Just when Jews first appeared in Rome we cannot tell. A Jewish embassy concluded a rather vague treaty with the Senate in 191 B.C.; and the fact that the Jews were expelled from Rome, together with the Chaldeans in 139 gives us a *terminus a quo*. By the end of the Republic they were numerous and influential, respected as so often by those whose respect is worth having, feared and hated by baser minds. It is recorded that at the funeral pyre of Julius Caesar no mourners were more assiduous than the Jews, for whom Julius, recognising their merits, had done so much. The moral standards of the Jews were far higher than those of the peoples among whom, since the days of the Ptolemies, they had been dispersed. The Ten Commandments not only set out, but enjoined, a standard of conduct far in advance of any contemporary set of sanctions, both in public and personal morals, including sexual attitudes and commercial transactions. To the original 'Mosaic' religion the sojourn 'beyond the River' during the Captivity in the sixth century B.C. had gradually added a whole new eschatology, for even after

the Return the ties between the two Jewries of Jerusalem and Babylon remained very close. It was from Babylon that the Jews brought back their concept of eternity and survival. The earliest Jewish idea of *Sheol*, the realm of the dead, is very little different from that of the Homeric underworld where the shadowy ghosts squeak like bats. The ghost of the prophet Samuel is but the puppet of the witch of Endor, to be raised at her whim. 'Shall they give thanks to thee in the pit?' asks the Psalmist.

In Babylon the Jews came in contact with, and rapidly adopted, a far different belief. As has already been said the Babylonian astronomers were famous. It happens that on the great plain of Mesopotamia, the 'plain of Shinar' of the Bible – so flat that in later days an Arab scientist would calculate a degree of the earth's circumference on it – the horizon is wider than anywhere else within thousands of miles. Also, the atmosphere is amazingly clear. The plain was therefore a natural observatory of which its inhabitants made good use at a very early date. By plotting the motions of the stars, they found that after a given period certain of them returned to the very same positions in the heavens. If they did this, argued the observers, they must be eternal. A fortiori, the power which had made them, and had set them in perpetual motion, must be even more eternal, if such an idea were conceivable.

Thus was born the concept of eternity, and of its corollary, eternal life. It deeply influenced Jewish thought. The conservative rabbinical school represented by the Sadducees 'which say there is no resurrection'

The more savage side of Mithraism is illustrated by this horrific deity, an *ex voto* of the year A.D. 190.

would have none of it; but it was eagerly promulgated by the so-called apocalyptic writers, who in their turn influenced the more liberal doctors. Of these apocalyptic writers the best known is the author of the Book of Daniel. To quote the late Dr Bevan in the CAH (Vol. viii, p. 512): 'The Jewish apocalypses ... differ from the older Hebrew prophecy in giving a formal scheme of world history: a succession of epochs are distinguished in the fight between good and evil up to the final triumph of good and the coming of the kingdom of God. It is likely that we may see here the influence of Persian Zoroastrianism. The chief importance of this literature in the development of Hebraic religion is that it spread among the Jews a new belief in life after death for the individual.' In the Book of Daniel, although there is no proclamation of a general resurrection, it is clear that certain deserving souls will attain immortality, (rather as Cicero was later to assert): 'Many of them that sleep in the dust of the earth shall awake, some to everlasting life, and some to shame and everlasting contempt. And they that be wise shall shine as the brightness of the firmament' – note the significant simile – 'and they shall turn many to righteousness *as the stars for ever and ever.*' (Daniel XII, 2 & 3.)

This book was written in or about the year 166 B.C.. just at a time when Jewish colonies were being established in Asia Minor where Jewry and Judaism were to exercise a profound influence. The story of Asian Jewry, although of the greatest interest, is outside the scope of this study: it will be enough to remark that among its sons was to be the Roman citizen,

Jewish scholar and Christian apostle Saul of Tarsus. What concerns us here is the influence of that Jewry on religion as it affected Rome.

Judaism's earliest contact with Rome may have been indirect, but none the less potent for that. Many of those among whom the Jews had settled were attracted by the newcomer's religion. Without wishing to become Jews, to observe all the injunctions and taboos of the Mosaic Law and so to become members of a separatist community, they did nevertheless come to infuse Jewish ideas into their own cults. Syncretist sects sprang up, in which Jewish and pagan ideas became intermingled, as we know from magical texts which often present us with the Yahweh of the Jews alongside Egyptian or Greek deities. We even find Attis addressed by the epithet reserved for the Jewish God, 'most high'.

It was in Asia Minor that this reciprocal mingling was most noticeable, and that in connection with a god very close to Attis and often confounded with him. His name was Sabazios. 'This ancient divinity of Thraco-Phrygian tribes', says Cumont, 'was by an audacious etymology, which goes back to the Hellenistic epoch, identified with Yahweh Sabaoth, the Lord of Hosts of the Bible. The *kyrios Sabaoth* of the Septuagint was regarded as the equivalent of the *kyrios Sabazios* of the Barbarians.'

Thus indirectly, no less than directly, Rome received the benediction of the God of Jacob. By the time of the Empire, we find an *haute Juiverie* established in Rome. Poppaea, Nero's empress, favoured the Jews, and it was through a Jewish actor who was

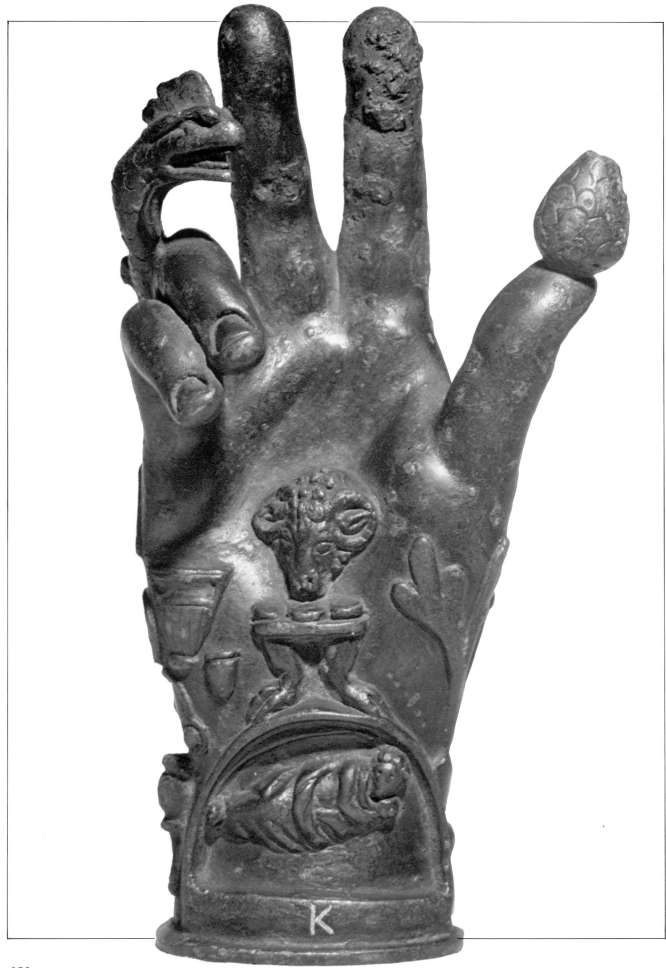

one of her favourites that the great Jewish historian Josephus obtained the *entreé*. It was a Jewish prince, Agrippa, grandson of Herod the Great, who was largely instrumental in securing the elevation of Claudius to the purple. Queen Berenice, Agrippa's daughter, captivated the future emperor Titus. It was this Jewry, so diverse and penetrating, that was to be the matrix of the first Christian church in Rome, founded by two immigrant Jews, named Peter and Paul.

The Persians

But not only from Palestine was the religion of Rome to receive new vigour: Persia too was to make her contribution. The relations between Persia and the west make one of the most arresting and one of the saddest studies in all ancient history. In our own day the Levant has become the scene of a struggle as sharp as it is barren between east and west. So it was in antiquity. For a whole millennium the ruinous feud went on. It is hard for us to gauge just what happened because, although they excelled in every art from architecture to jewelry, the ancient Persians have left us no literature whatever. We are forced, therefore, to take our facts from Greek and Roman historians, helped out here and there by massive Persian rock-carvings. Even so, it is clear that Persia was almost continuously a powerful, often a dominating, force in the politics of the Levant and of her neighbours. In the sixth century B.C. Persia became lord of Babylonia and Assyria, that is of southern and northern Mesopotamia, and then of

Lydia and Ionia. The Levant and Egypt followed. Only mainland Hellas escaped the Persian yoke, saved by the heroes of Marathon, Salamis and Plataea, and even then only at the cost of the destruction of the Acropolis of Athens.

One hundred and fifty years later Alexander destroyed the empire of the Achaemenids, and carried hellenistic culture to the banks of the Indus. Then, after another two and a half centuries, the Iranian tide swept back. The Parthian Arsacids reached the confines of Syria, and a supposed descendant of Darius called Mithradates Eupator at the head of the nobility of Pontus penetrated to the heart of Hellas. By now Rome was the lord of the ascendant, and the Parthians were compelled to retire, but not before they had inflicted on Rome one of the most humiliating defeats in all Roman history.

Yet again they were to show their resilient might. In the third century A.D. the Sassanians revived the old Persian power; and from then until the triumphant explosion of Islam, Rome and Persia continuously and ruinously fought each other, with one Roman emperor meeting his death as the captive of the Persians and another being killed on the field of battle.

The extraordinary vitality of the Persians was due to their moral and intellectual qualities. Not a few Greeks were captivated by them. Themistokles, the saviour of Athens, ended his days as a Persian satrap. Fifty years later, Alkibiades died as an exile in Persian Phrygia. Xenophon, the pupil of Socrates, already mentioned in connection with Zeno, was a volunteer in and later leader of a Greek expeditionary force which went to the aid of the Persian prince Cyrus in 401 B.C. Later on, living in retirement in Southern Greece not far from Olympia, he decided to write a little manual on how to bring up a gentleman. He called it 'The Childhood of Cyrus', because it was the Persians who in his experience had all the gentlemanly virtues. Their children were taught to ride, to shoot and to tell the truth, just as English boys

once were.

This vigorous civilisation never became assimilated to Hellenism as in varying degrees the Aryans of Phrygia, the Semites of the Levant and the Hamites of Egypt did. Hellas and Persia were two adversaries of equal nobility – what a Persian ambassador described to a Roman emperor of the fourth century as 'the two eyes of the human race'. Alexander the Great had intended to blend these twin forces into one beneficent whole, as being the only two 'master-races' worthy of ruling Asia. He failed; and the two peoples relapsed into their traditional antagonism. It was nevertheless inevitable that an association, however bitter, of more than a thousand years should beget some mutual exchanges. Persian customs, Persian systems of administration, were adopted by Alexander's successors, and so passed to Rome. The Caesars, for instance, were preceded on official occasions by an officer who carried the sacred fire, the symbol of perpetual authority, just as Darius had been. Moreover, they gradually came to regard themselves, after the manner of Artaxerxes, as the sacrosanct masters of the world.

Persian religion, like Persian customs, had spread far and wide, and it had done so by the same means as Judaism had, through the little islands and colonies of Iranian settlers and traders. Backed by the military, artistic and political prestige of its country of origin, the Persian cult was destined to be the most widely diffused, most popular and most enduring of all the pagan religions which Rome embraced, until at the end of the third century A.D. the emperor Diocletian would hail Mithras, the Persian god, as the protector of the reorganised empire. Even when Mithras was dethroned by Christianity it lived on in dignified opposition by becoming a Christian heresy, namely Manichaeism, which right down to the Middle Ages was to be a source of strife and bloodshed.

To this day there is visible in London, within a bowshot (say, 500 metres) of St Paul's cathedral, the remnants of a temple of Mithras.

103

Above. Bas-relief found at Vénasque. It shows the head of Mithras, wearing a Phrygian bonnet, surmounting the sun, and flanked by two lions representing the fourth degree of initiation. Baptistery, Vénasque.

Opposite above. A bust of Mithras found in the excavation of the Walbrook Mithraeum, London, in 1954. It was made in Italy *c.* A.D. 200 and imported into Britain. Museum of London.

Opposite below. Two coins of the Kushan dynasty (which ruled in Central Asia and northern India during the 1st and 2nd centuries A.D.) showing Mithra (Mithras) with radiate crown, tunic, mantle and short boots. In the left coin he carries a sword and torque; in the right he carries a staff and holds out his hand, perhaps in blessing.

Mithras

What were the origins of this potent deity? Alas, we know hardly anything about them. That Mithras was a Persian god we do know. But how did he make his way from the highlands of Iran to Italy? Plutarch, as so often, is of some help. He tells us that Pompey, in the year 67 B.C., when he was hunting down the pirates, found that they used to offer strange sacrifices on the top of a volcano in Lycia (in southern Asia Minor) and celebrate secret rites – among them those of Mithras 'which have been preserved to our own day, having been originally taught by them'. Pompey's own action must have helped in the propagation of this faith, because unlike Julius Caesar who crucified pirates when he caught them, Pompey settled them on the land, as far as possible from the tempting sea, not only in Asia but in Greece and even in southern Italy as well. An obscure Latin author commenting on a line by an earlier poet says the cult of Mithras passed from the Persians to the Phrygians and from the Phrygians to the Romans. Thus, both Plutarch and the scholiast give Asia Minor as the launching-pad, as it were, of Mithraism. Other evidence supports them. One king Mithradates has been mentioned: the name frequently occurs in the dynasties not only of Pontus, but of Cappadocia, Armenia and Commagene, proof of the devotion of these pretended Achaemenid dynasties to Mithras. A famous rock-relief in Commagene shows king Antiochus I (first century B.C.) shaking hands with Mithras, whose head is surrounded with a nimbus and with solar rays, and who wears the familiar Phrygian cap.

The Mithraic cult with which the Romans came in contact in the days of Pompey had developed in Anatolia during the previous century: just how, we cannot be precise.

But this we know: when the Persians occupied Asia Minor, they found there, as Strabo assures us, a climate such as they were used to at home, and a terrain admirably suited to the breeding of horses. We have already seen how much the Persians

Above. The cult of Mithras spread as far north as Northumberland. This temple of Mithras is at Carrowburgh. (Concrete pillars have replaced the original wooden ones).

Opposite. The Anatolian deity, Men, seen with a thyrsis in his right hand and a pine cone in the left. His foot rests on the head of a bull. The inscription reads: 'Agathapous of Kaouala offers his prayer to Men'. This work of the second century A.D. is an interesting synthesis of Dionysiac and Mithraic symbolism. Museum of London.

Right. The Mithraeum beneath the church of S. Clemente, near the Colosseum. The vault is so constructed as to represent a cave. It was adorned with mosaics. On the front of the altar, Mithras is slaying the bull. In the background (right) is a bust of the sun-god, wearing his radiate crown. Third or fourth century A.D.

Opposite. One of the two tasks facing Mithras in his trial of strength with the Sun-god was the capture of a wild bull, which he later sacrificed. From the creature's body sprang many gifts useful to man. The depiction of the slaying of the bull was a common theme in Roman Mithraic temples. Musée du Louvre, Paris.

---

respected horsemanship; and they had developed a system of cavalry both heavy and light which were the ancient analogues of the tank and the aeroplane respectively. So arose and flourished a feudal aristocracy, rather like the Norman knights, which preserving the hereditary Persian title of 'satrap', remained masters of their fiefs until the days of Justinian in the sixth century. They worshipped Mithras as the guardian of their arms, and that is why even in the Latin world Mithras endured as the patron-in-chief of soldiers and armies.

Celebrated temples, served by a numerous clergy, arose in profusion, just as in later days sumptuous cathedrals would burgeon in Mexico and in Goa in the wake of devout warriors. Magi, or 'fire-bearers', were to be found all over the Levant. Prayers and hymns were chanted before the altar on which glowed the sacred flame, milk and honey and oil were offered, with the same precautions taken as in Persia lest the breath of the officiant should sully the holy fire.

What was it that caused Mithraism to attract so many votaries throughout the Roman world? Its rites, celebrated in caves and crypts were not nearly as poignant or exciting as those of Cybele or Isis. Purification, a sort of baptism, a common meal, these could be found elsewhere, and celebrated with far more grandeur. The revolting rite of the *taurobolium*, that is, the drenching of a neophyte crouching in a pit with the blood of a bull slaughtered above him, as a symbol of regeneration, though frequently associated with Mithras the Bullslayer is properly a rite not of Mithraism but of the Great Mother of Asia Minor.

The revelation of Mithras, the lord of light, surrounded by the signs of the Zodiac representing the heavens, slaying a bull, the living embodiment of brute force at its strongest – that would not alone have sufficed to make Mithras supreme. What Persia brought to religion was a *capital principle*: dualism.

'It was this that set Mithraism quite apart from the other cults, and inspired its dogmatic and moral teaching, giving them a stiffening and a stability hitherto unknown in Roman paganism. It presented the universe under an aspect unknown before and at the same time provided a new aim for existence.'

Right is right and wrong is wrong. Both are living spirits, and so both must be conciliated. Ahura-Mazda is the spirit of light, Ahriman the spirit of darkness. Ahura-Mazda, Mithras, the Sun-god – they easily coalesce. So do Ahriman and Satan. The propitiation of the devil has lasted down to our own day among the Yezidis of northern Iraq; and it was from Persia that Judaism received and bequeathed to Christianity its concept of the Evil One.

This theoretical explanation of the universe, however satisfying, would not of itself serve to make a religion prevail. 'Conduct', as Matthew Arnold remarked, 'is three-quarters of life.' And it was in the regulation of conduct that Mithras excelled. It laid upon its adherents definite 'commandments', though we do not know what they were. Mithras exalted brotherhood as well. One class of his initiates was known as 'soldiers', just as Christians were exhorted by St Paul to be. This spirit of military discipline appealed to traditional Roman ethics, and breathed a new vigour into western paganism. God of light, spirit of truth and justice – Mithras was all of these. He was, in addition, the god of loyalty to one's word: an oath sanctioned by him was considered to be inviolable.

What a change from the lush mysteries of the Nile or of Phrygia! This chaste, celibate god commends not the reckless fertility of nature but the single-minded continence of the spirit.

Of all the eastern cults no other offered so rigorous a system as that of Mithras. Is it to be wondered at that in Britain alone, where only three Roman legions were stationed, no less than five temples of Mithras have come to light? No other religion was so morally elevated nor secured such a hold on men's hearts and souls. Renan's famous *mot* has often been repeated (it occurs in his *Marc-Aurèle*): 'If Christianity had been arrested in its growth by some mortal malady, the world would have been Mithraist.'

By the third century of our era, Mithraism had indeed become almost the official religion of the Empire. Even today in many contexts both Christian and 'humanist' we may catch echoes of that religion which was Persia's great spiritual gift to her material rival, Rome.

The Eternal City

With so many alien cults flourishing in Rome, it might well be supposed that in the latter days of the first century B.C. Roman religion as such perished as the Republic perished. In fact, it did nothing of the sort. On the contrary, the state religion was consolidated, and in so robust a form that it lasted for four centuries longer, outlived all the foreign importations except Judaism and Mithraism and only yielded in the end to Christianity.

This remarkable rejuvenation was primarily the work of an emperor and some poets, an alliance more reminiscent of China than workaday Rome. Even in this inquisitive age there are fortunately some questions which cannot be answered, and one of them is why genius blossoms when and where it does. It happened that in the closing years of the Republic, when the Roman polity was falling into utter ruin, Rome produced the greatest poets she was ever to nurture, two of them among the greatest the world has ever seen. Publius Virgilius Maro, or Virgil, was born near Mantua in the year 70 B.C., twenty years after Lucretius, by whose work Virgil was to be profoundly influenced, and seventeen years after Catullus, whom Virgil imitated in his earlier poems. Five years younger than Virgil was Quintus Horatius Flaccus, who was to be his close friend. Albius Tibullus was born in 54, Sextus Propertius in 49 and Publius Ovidius Naso in 43. Of this galaxy, Ovid has already been mentioned. His contribution to religion was, it may be said, involuntary. He was a brilliant rake: as he put it himself, 'I see the better and am all for it: I follow the worse'. He was banished by Augustus to the Black Sea for some unknown offence, presumably sexual.

It is on these seven poets that the fame of Latin poetry chiefly rests, all of them born within fifty years. Any history of Latin literature must pay detailed homage to each one of them. For our purposes Catullus and Propertius are hardly relevant, though the former wrote a wonderful poem called *Attis*, in which he gives a glittering account of that deity's solemnities. Tibullus is notable for his devotion to the old rural religion and has bequeathed to us several descriptions of rural rites in charming verse.

Augustus

Of the great revival, social and religious, which was to generate what we still call the Augustan age, the mainspring was political, the work of the emperor himself. Augustus cannot be described as a religious man. In his youth he had been callously brutal, just as his contemporaries were. He had even consented to the murder of Cicero. To the end of his days he could be unfeelingly harsh in his dealings with his family. He would compel spouses who dearly loved each other to divorce for dynastic reasons; he would banish his daughter, he would barter his sister for a political accommodation. Yet his public character did beyond question develop and enlarge, so much so that people sought to explain the transformation by some divine intervention.

When Julius Caesar was assassinated on 15 March 44 B.C., it was found that he had named as his heir an obscure great-nephew called Octavian. He was only nineteen, and physically weak; but he was a prudent and determined youth, and he

Dougga. When the Romans established
cities in their overseas empire, they took
their gods with them. Thus, in Dougga,
Tunisia, we find a temple dedicated to the
Roman triad of the Capitol. Jupiter, Juno
and Minerva.

Above. Augustus, Julius Caesar's great-nephew and adopted son and heir, the creator of the Roman empire. This head shows him as he liked to be regarded, calm, far-seeing, firm and benevolent; no king, but the leader and guide of his people.

Top right. Ara Pacis, south side. Flamens, Agrippa (veiled, as all officiants habitually were) Julia his wife, daughter of Augustus, Tiberius and Lucius Caesar. These are all real people, in their habits as they were, including the little child, who would clearly rather be elsewhere playing with his hoop.

Centre right. The Ara Pacis, or Altar of Peace, as it appears today, reassembled opposite the mausoleum of Augustus. It was erected between 13 and 9 B.C. to celebrate the peace established throughout the Roman world after the return of Augustus from Spain and Gaul. It marks the peak of Roman art, and is a powerful exposition of Roman religious ideas.

Bottom right. Part of a frieze from the Ara Pacis showing members of the Imperial family and officiants in procession.

Opposite. Roma was a goddess who represented the Eternal City. She is seen here with priests and soldiers.

had some outstandingly gifted friends. At first he worked with Mark Antony, to whom his saintly sister Octavia was at one time married, after the death of her first husband Marcellus. In the end Antony's jealousy and his corroding passion for Cleopatra caused an irreparable rift. At the battle of Actium in 31 B.C. Antony and Cleopatra were defeated and fled to Egypt where they took their own lives. That meant that Oc-

tavian was now master of the Roman world. It meant, too, that the Roman world, after a century of sordid and devastating strife, was to know peace. Having achieved this so long despaired of boon, Augustus set about revivifying the spirit of Rome and the Romans. His object was to revive the old Roman virtues, the virtues which had made Rome great, the virtues of Camillus, of the Scipios, of Cato. His own contribution to the Reformation

was impressive. He restored no less than eighty-two temples. In the year 13 B.C. he erected on the Campus Martius a wonderful memorial called the *Ara Pacis*, the Altar of Peace, which has of recent years been almost miraculously reassembled. Let us now take a close look at this masterpiece in stone with Professor Jocelyn Toynbee.

'The Ara Pacis expresses a more intimate sense of history [than earlier sculpture], a deeper devotion to fact and actuality, in presenting contemporary, living people, some of them individuals whose identity we can fix with certainty, or with a very high degree of probability, caught in marble, just as they were at a given moment, on 4 July 13 B.C. The south side is occupied by the emperor himself, with his immediate entourage of officials, priests and relations, the north side by members of the Roman

Right. Cameo, by Dioscorides, of Augustus whose rule marked the founding of the Roman Empire. British Museum, London.

Opposite. Bacchus, the god of wine, clothed appropriately in grapes, stands with Mount Vesuvius in the background. Museo Archeologico Nazionale, Naples.

Below. Ara Pacis, west side. Aeneas, Augustus's prototype, sacrificing to Juno the white sow which was the augury for his founding of Lavinium, a thanksgiving for his homecoming to the promised land of Italy.

religious fraternities, magistrates, senators, and other persons, with their families, who walked behind. On the east side facing the great highway, are two groups of personifications symbolising to all passers-by the far-reaching and enduring effects of the *Pax Romana* now solemnly established by Augustus's return [he had been on an extensive tour of the western provinces] – the warrior goddess Roma, seated at peace, and Tellus, or more probably the motherland of Italy, rich in children and in all the other gifts which peace bestows. On the west side are two legendary scenes – Aeneas, Augustus's prototype, making his sacrifice, that offered to Juno, of the famous white sow of the prodigy, the augury for the foundation of Lavinium, a sacrifice for his home-coming to the promised land of Italy;

Above. Ara Pacis, detail showing a suovetaurilia.

Opposite. A statue of the Emperor Augustus Caesar who ruled 44 B.C.–A.D. 14 reflects the imperial dignity of his rule. Musei Vaticani.

Below. Ara Pacis, east side, Mother Earth, or perhaps Italy, rich in children and other gifts of peace, from land, sea and sky.

and the scene of the Lupercal, where in the presence of Mars and Faustulus, the (now vanished) she-wolf suckled Romulus and his brother. . . . The Ara Pacis appeals to us by its serene tranquillity, its unpretentious stateliness, its homely intimacy, its gracious informality, its delight in Nature, its purposeful unity, and not least by its modest dimensions. It embodies the very best that Rome bestowed on Italy and it strikes that perfect balance between land and city on which Augustus claimed to build his empire.'

In this great enterprise, Augustus's two ministers, Agrippa and Maecenas, were his willing instruments. Agrippa, whom Buchan characterised as 'the supreme example in history of a man of the first order whom loyalty constrained to take the second place', was a brilliant general. It was he who enabled Octavian, or Augustus as he was soon called, to create the peace which the poets praised. Agrippa did not himself care for poets or their works: he even went so far as to criticise Virgil for plagiarism at a time when everyone else was lauding him. Maecenas, though not so great a man as Agrippa, was the link between Augustus and the literary world, so that his name has become a synonym for enlightened patronage of the arts. He was descended from Etruscan kings, a knight who never cared to become a senator, and a close friend of Virgil and Horace, as they were of each other. This trio, Maecenas, Virgil and Horace, were to have a deep and abiding influence not only on the literary patrimony of Rome but on the life of its citizens.

Horace

Here we are concerned only with the contributions to the religious revival

Above. An astrological globe showing various figures representing the constellations.

Opposite. The poet Virgil is seen seated between two Muses, Clio (History) and Melpomene (Tragedy). He is holding the *Aeneid* open at Book 1, of which line 11 reads: 'O Muse the causes and the crimes relate, What Goddess was provoked and whence her hate'. Mosaic from Sousse, Tunisia, second-third century A.D. Musée National du Bardo, Tunis.

which the Augustan age was to witness at the bidding of the emperor and his ministers and poets. Virgil and Horace although linked by bonds of true affection were utterly different in character. Both claimed to be Epicureans; but whereas Virgil had for six years been a pupil of Siro, a well-known and highly respected teacher who conducted his 'Garden' in Campania, Horace admits that he was no more than a 'sleek pig in Epicurus's herd'. Nevertheless he played his part in the revival. He felt it his duty to do so. After all, his friends Maecenas and Augustus – and they were true and loyal friends – had been very good to him and had enabled him to lead a life of comfort and leisure on his beloved Sabine farm. Augustus had even wanted Horace to be his secretary and was not offended when Horace declined the offer. No one ever commended morals with more elegance or less conviction than Horace. This he did in the so-called Roman odes of his third book. He sent forth beautifully phrased appeals for the restoration of and return to the temples (which Horace seldom entered), for the abatement of luxury (which Horace loved) and for the general bracing of morals (which Horace preferred unbraced). He did something else as well. As part of his campaign of Renewal, Augustus decided in 17 B.C. to revive the secular games.

just at this time that the Ambarvalia used to go round the ripening crops, and that the *penus* of Vesta was cleaned to receive the new grain. Augustus realised how important agriculture and the old yeoman stock that lived by it were to Rome, specially in a day when the citizens were supplied with free doles of imported corn; indeed, it was to offset this dependence and to help repair the ravages of the civil wars that Augustus and Virgil with him did their utmost to restore the dignity of the farmer.

On the night before the first of June Augustus and Agrippa sacrificed to the Fates, mentioned in Horace's hymn, on the second night to the Greek deity of childbirth, Eilythia, and on the third to Mother Earth. Rome's ruler prayed for the prosperity of Rome, and also for himself and his family. 'The scene on the bank of the Tiber, illuminated by torches, must have been most impressive.' Daylight, too, had its rites. On the first two days Augustus and Agrippa offered the appropriate sacrifices to Jupiter and Juno on the Capitol. On the third and last day the focus was transferred to the Palatine, where Augustus lived, and where he had built his grand temple to Apollo. And here was sung Horace's hymn. It is, like many laureate effusions, formal and rather cold. It extols Rome, invokes a company of gods and goddesses, prays for young and old, lauds public and private virtues. It was sung by twenty-seven (three times three times three) boys and the same number of maidens who had both parents living. The company then left the Palatine, processed down the Sacred Way, through the Forum

Virgil had died two years before, so it naturally fell to Horace as unofficial laureate to compose an ode for what was to be a grand national festival of unity.

The *Ludi Saeculares* take their name from the word *saeculum*, which meant originally a period stretching from any given moment to the death of the oldest person born at that moment, that is, roughly a century. A new saeculum could thus begin at any time. Augustus decided that, in the year 17, a new leaf had been turned over in the history of the city, and that the citizens must be convinced of

the fact by some impressive exercises. The programme for the festival was elaborate, and by good fortune we know quite a lot about it. On 26 May and the two following days materials for purification, torches, sulphur and bitumen, were distributed by the priests to all free inhabitants of Rome, whether citizens or not. Even bachelors, who had recently been banned from public entertainments, were to be admitted. During the next three days, the people came before the College of Fifteen, the Quindecemviri, and offered firstfruits, as is done today at harvest festivals. It was

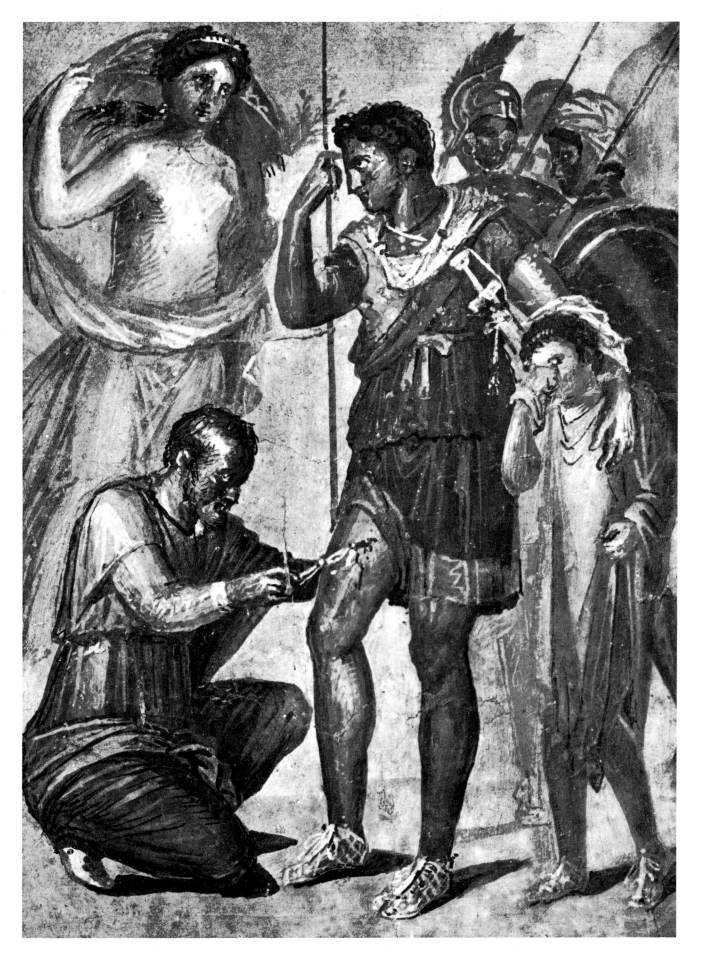

and up to the Capitol on the other side, where the hymn was repeated. 'It is', says the *Cambridge Ancient History* 'in a peculiarly Roman way an alliance of the throne and altar, and such an alliance means that the altar is not at the time in question a political creation devoid of significance.' The general impression must have been like that of an Albert Hall youth rally singing 'Land of Hope and Glory'.

The ode contained a graceful reference to the *Aeneid* of Virgil.

Virgil

When we turn from Horace to Virgil, we turn from charm to genius, from the urbane to the spiritual. Virgil is quite unlike any other Roman of whom we have record, unlike almost any other poet. His position in world literature is accurately described by Dryden in his famous epigram:

Three poets in three distant ages born,
Greece, Italy and England did adorn.
The first in loftiness of thought surpassed,
The next in majesty, in both the last.
The force of nature could no further go,
To make a third she joined the other two.

Homer, Virgil, Milton – such is the exalted triad. Majesty: that is the theme of Virgil, and it is a spiritual majesty. In considering Virgil's religion it is well once more to remind ourselves that dogmatic belief was unknown to Greece or Rome. To our own age, whether we belong to any church or to none, religion is a matter of dogma, of a faith once and for all delivered, crystallised in a Torah, a Nicene creed, a Koran, hedged and interpreted by a hierarchy. Roman religion, as we have seen, was nothing of the sort: it was a collection of formulae, more the child of the lawcourt than of the shrine. The individual Roman's religion was his own concern: he could believe or disbelieve, pick and choose as he liked. Virgil as

Nereids with a sea-monster. From a mosaic of Lambaesis, Algeria.

The River God Tiber reclining, with two female attendants. Fresco from Pompeii. Musée du Louvre, Paris.

Above. Juturna taking leave of her brother Turnus, a relief from her altar in the Forum.

Opposite. Dido, queen of Carthage, abandoned by Aeneas, whose ship is seen at the top of this Pompeian fresco. In Roman eyes, Aeneas was only doing his duty as a patriot, because Carthage, the hereditary foe, had so very recently been reincarnated in another oriental queen, Cleopatra.

already noted started as an Epicurean, because that retiring code of conduct suited his temperament. He was a man of almost feminine delicacy and sensitivity. He never married. When he lived near Naples he was called Parthenias, a happy blending of the old name of the city, Parthenope, and the Greek word Parthenos, virgin, which his own name so nearly resembles. (By a strange analogy, Milton when at Cambridge was called, on account of his beauty, 'the lady of Christ's'.) In Virgil's poetry there are traces of Orphic belief and of Neopythagorean philosophy; but it is his own elevation of mind and soul that has made it immortal. Not all of Virgil is easily intelligible by any means. In fact he seems to have intended to withhold much of what he felt, as it were

through spiritual shyness, from the vulgar. Sometimes he appears to have deliberately used ambiguity to give the effect of a 'double-take'. When Aeneas describes his journey towards his goal, Italy, he says he 'grasps fleeting shores', a phrase which in the original can mean either that the shores were fleeting or that he was. Surely he meant both? Again in a line of the Fourth Eclogue, he bids the wonder-child begin to recognise his mother with a smile: the Latin can mean either that the mother is smiling or the child. Again, it is easier to understand that each is smiling at the other. Sometimes the language is used for its own sake, to paint a picture in sound. 'Suadentque cadentia sidera somnum' – 'the setting stars counsel sleep'. Here the sound suggests the meaning, as it does of the souls in the underworld who stretch forth their hands through longing for the other side: 'Tendebantque manus ripae ulterioris amore'. But there are lines which cannot be translated at all. 'Sunt lacrimae rerum, mentem et mortalia tangunt.' 'There are tears of things, and what is mortal touches the mind.' We can transmute these banal syllables into sense and pathos only by using Virgil's own spiritual code. Tennyson in the ode which he wrote for the nineteen-hundredth anniversary of Virgil's birth perfectly expresses this essence-like quality of Virgil when he refers to 'all the charm of all the Muses, Often flowering in a lonely word'.

The Aeneid

Virgil's contemporaries at once understood how great he was. His *Eclogues*, specially the Fourth, had established his reputation; his *Georgics* increased it. His *Aeneid* was awaited with eager awe. Propertius wrote: 'Give place, Roman writers, Greek writers too: something greater than the *Iliad* is coming to birth'. The *Aeneid* was written book by book, and was in fact never finished. Virgil had asked that it might be destroyed after his death; but Augustus overruled him – the most beneficial imperial veto ever exercised. He had heard some of the poem. When Virgil

had read the sixth book to Augustus and his sister Octavia, and came to the passage wherein he makes Aeneas's father foretell the birth of Octavia's son Marcellus, who had recently died, the stricken mother swooned – though fortunately she came to in time to give Virgil a nice present.

Dante chose Virgil to be his guide in his journey through the afterworld. The reason for Virgil's reputation in the Christian world rests less on the elevation of mind which Dryden praises than on two poems, one early, the other late, namely the Fourth Eclogue and the sixth book of the Aeneid. The Fourth Eclogue is addressed to a friend, Asinius Pollio, whom Virgil hails as the 'only begetter' of his Eclogues, and foretells the birth of a wonderful child who is to usher in the golden age. No one knows whether Virgil had in mind any particular child, or whether he was giving utterance to a general hope that a new age was dawning, as indeed it was. Both Virgil and Pollio may easily have been acquainted with Hebrew Messianic writings, and with the concept of a regeneration of mankind.

Certain it is that the Fourth Eclogue was received from the earliest days of Christianity as a prophecy of the birth of Christ, which occurred less than forty years after it was written. Constantine expressly invokes the authority of the Fourth Eclogue in the speech in which he decreed that Christianity was henceforth to be the religion of the Roman state. The Virgilian legend grew and proliferated throughout the Middle Ages; but that aspect of Virgil is outside the scope of the present study. Virgil's influence on specifically *Roman* thought derives far more from the *Aeneid* than from the *Eclogues*. Here, at last, is a genuinely Roman myth, a true product of Roman genius, expounding the greatness and destiny of Rome. The story, certainly as old as the fifth century B.C. as we know from an Etruscan terracotta now in the Villa Giulia in Rome, is that of Aeneas the good, who flees from burning Troy with his old father Anchises. Anchises dies,

Aeneas is carried to Libya, where he becomes the lover of Dido, queen of Carthage. Urged by his destiny and his duty, he leaves Dido, who kills herself. Eventually Aeneas reaches Latium. Aided by the Sibyl of Cumae, he visits the underworld where he sees Dido, meets his father and is shown the souls of many who are to come after him, including the darling Marcellus. He is entertained by Evander on the site of what will one day be Rome. Venus sends Aeneas a shield wrought by Vulcan on which are depicted scenes from future Roman history, including Augustus's victory at Actium and the worldwide empire of Rome. The Tuscans, led by Turnus, oppose Aeneas. After bitter struggles Aeneas is victorious. He marries Lavinia, a local princess, and settles in Latium, where he and his men will

thereafter be known not as Trojans but as Latins.

This story, with all its many adventures, told in incomparable verse, at once became the bible of Rome. Romans of all classes knew it by heart. It glorified Rome, it showed how 'gravitas', 'pietas', 'dignitas' were the supreme virtues, how passionate love such as that of Aeneas for Dido, in other words, that of Antony for Cleopatra, could in the end lead only to ruin. The gods, Fate which sometimes overruled even gods, the supernatural solicitings of the Sibyl, the afterworld, duty to neighbour and state – all here are woven into one great tapestry without seam. Above all, the imperial destiny of Rome is foreshadowed. At the end of the sixth book Anchises utters his famous prophecy, which Dryden

renders as follows:

Let others better mould the running Mass
Of Metals, and inform the breathing Brass;
And soften into flesh a Marble Face:
Plead better at the Bar; describe the Skies,
And when the Stars descend and when they rise.
But Rome, 'tis thine alone, with awful sway
To rule mankind, and make the World obey;
Disposing Peace, and War, thy own majestic Way,
To tame the Proud, the fetter'd Slave to free;
These are Imperial Arts, and worthy thee.

Virgil's achievement in the realm of

religion is brilliantly summed up by Pierre Boyancé in his *La Réligion de Virgile* (Paris 1963):

'Virgil expresses his time and his country. His time, by yoking the voluntary return to the traditions of the past with the welcome given to all that seemed best in the Greek message: the beauty of poetry, the truth of philosophy. His country, in the fact that Rome had always been from its earliest days very shut and very open. Very shut, by its overweening confidence in the superiority of its moral vigour and piety. Very open by a certainty no less strong that the gods had given to others gifts which it was important to turn to advantage. . . . It is impossible at one and the same time to admire Virgil and to condemn Rome. For posterity he is Rome's most fervent, but also most faithful, interpreter. . . . It is above all the Fourth Eclogue, it is above all the sixth book of the *Aeneid*, which was bound to give to Virgil in the eyes of posterity something of the inspired prophet. It was these verses which Christianity was bound to hold to because it found in them something of its own revelation. In them Virgil gives us the impression of rising above his time and his country. . . . He alone knew how to weld the history of Rome into that of the whole of humanity, in which the cosmos itself took a part. In that is expressed the very depth of his soul, and there souls are not deceived: he had the honour of guiding Dante to the threshold of Paradise.'

Rome, the Eternal City, situated on the banks of the Tiber and surrounded by protective hills. By the time she had reached her hey-day, Rome had accumulated many impressive monuments and temples. For example, Augustus built a new *Forum Augustum*, a palace on the Palatine and three new aqueducts, and erected many other monuments. Very often these building programmes were at the cost of living space and the common people continued to dwell in crowded and insanitary conditions. Great fires offered the only chance of rebuilding in the older regions.

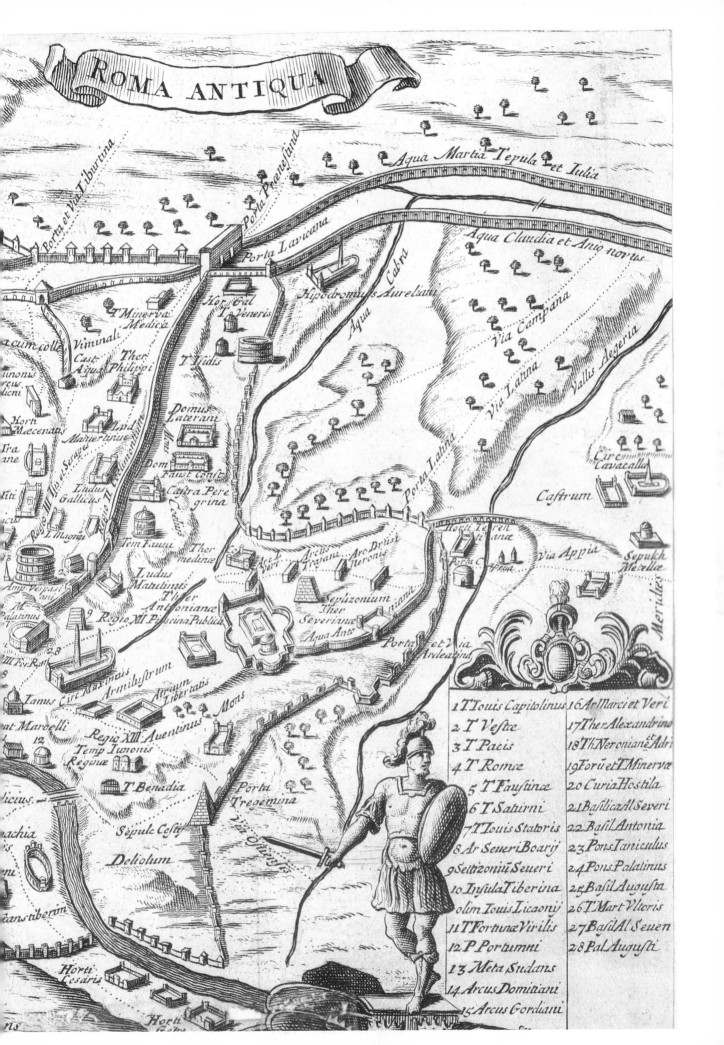

ROMA ANTIQUA

Aqua Martia Tepula et Iulia

Aqua Claudia et Anio novus

Porta et Via Tiburtina

Porta Praenestina

Porta Lavicana

Cabra

Aqua

Via Campana

Via Latina

Vallis Aegeria

Hipodromus Aurelianus

Hor Gal T Veneris

T Minerva Medica

Viminali

Cast Aqua Philippi

Ther Philippi

T Isidis

Domus Laterani

Circ Cavacalla

Castrum

cum colle

unonis reus deni

Horti Macenatis

Trane

Manertinus

Lud.

Dom

Faust Const

Castra Peregrina

Caelius

Porta Latina

Horti Terentiana

Via Appia

Sepulch Metella

Titi

cus

Ludus Gallicus Regio III Hir. et Serapes

Reg II Dolmentius

T L Magnus

Tem Fauni

Ther medinie

Arc T Veri

Arcus Trajani

Arc Drusi Neronis

Porta Capena

Meridies

Ther Antoniance

Ludus Matutinus

Sepizonium

Ther Severiance

Aqua Ant

nianis

Amp Vespasiani

M Palatinus

Regio XII Piscina Publica

Porta et Via Ardeatina

VIII Por Rom

Circ Maximis

Armilustrum

Atrium Libertatis

Mons

Tanus

Regio XIII Auentinus

at Marcelli

Temp Iunonis Reginae

12

T Benadia

Portu Tregemina

lacus.

Sepulc Cestij

Via Ostiensis

achia

Deliolum

us.

ans tiberim

Horti Cesaris

ns

Horti Cesta

1 T Iouis Capitolinus	16 Ar Marci et Veri
2 T Vestae	17 Ther Alexandrino
3 T Pacis	18 Th Neroniane et Adri
4 T Romae	19 Foru et T Minerva
5 T Faustinae	20 Curia Hostila
6 T Saturni	21 Basilica Al Severi
7 T Iouis Statoris	22 Basil Antonia
8 Ar Seueri Boarij	23 Pons Ianiculus
9 Settizoniu Seueri	24 Pons Palatinus
10 Insula Tiberina	25 Basil Augusta
olim Iouis Licaonij	26 T Mart Vltoris
11 T Fortunae Virilis	27 Basil Al Seuen
12 P Portumni	28 Pal Augusti
13 Meta Sudans	
14 Arcus Domitiani	
15 Arcus Gordiani	

Christ and Caesar

Christianity

'La venue même du Christ n'a rien qui étonne quand on a lu Virgile.'

However surely the nineteenth century may have been in agreement with Sainte Beuve, the first most emphatically was not. On the contrary, while Virgil was being read by everyone, the coming of Christ caused the greatest possible astonishment.

Just when the Christian message first reached Rome we cannot say. It was of course intimately connected with Jewry. As we have seen, as early as 139 B.C. the Jews had been expelled from Rome 'for attempting', in the words of Valerius Maximus, 'to corrupt Roman morals by the cult of Jupiter Sabazios'. We have also seen how by the close of the Republic the Jews had gained favour and privilege from Rome's rulers. The emperor Gaius, who became Rome's third imperial ruler in A.D. 37, cancelled these indulgences. Claudius, who succeeded him in 41, at once restored them – he owed his elevation to the throne largely to his Jewish friend Agrippa – but in 49, says Suetonius, banished the Jews 'who at the instigation of Chrestus [that is, Christ] continually raised tumults'. From this passage we must infer that, as in Jerusalem and elsewhere, the majority of Jews rejected, and opposed those among them who accepted, the Christian faith, which maintained not only that the Messiah had appeared, but also that Gentiles might be admitted to his fellowship. From St Paul's letter to the Romans, written a few years later, it is clear that the Christian community in Rome contained a Gentile element, although the phenomenon of Christianity was still hardly recognised apart from Judaism. On the other hand by the time of the fire of A.D. 64, that is, four years after the arrival in Rome of Paul himself, the existence of Christians as such was well known in the city. Whether they were actually accused of being incendiaries is not certain, but that they were accused of being Christians and used by Nero as scapegoats for a disaster of which he and they were equally innocent is beyond question.

And all this within a generation of the crucifixion of Jesus of Nazareth. Why?

The answer is involved. That Virgil had elevated the Roman mind, and that the Roman mind had adopted Virgil, cannot be denied. In the words of the late T. R. Glover: 'Whenever we think of "that hard Roman world", we have to remember that it is the world of Virgil, and that it loved Virgil.' Every schoolboy read Virgil, idlers would scrawl Virgilian graffiti on the walls of Pompeii, lonely soldiers would adorn their barrack-rooms on distant frontiers with quotations from the *Aeneid*. Nor was Virgil to be the only elevating influence on Roman thought. In the next century, the two Senecas, father and son, of Spanish origin, would introduce into Roman life a new and lofty infusion of Stoicism. The contribution of the younger Seneca was to endure for centuries, and to inspire not only the first English dramatists but the very plots and concepts of Racine himself. Yes, there was beyond cavil much in the claim made by the best Romans of the early empire that they really were better than their predecessors. And yet it took three centuries for the Christian faith to win acceptance and in the end to coalesce with what was best in the pagan world.

Christianity and the State

The reasons for the state's opposition to the new religion are complex and its attitude to it oscillated between tolerance and persecution. There was of course no objection to it on what we should call religious grounds, because as we have seen the individual Roman's religion was his own affair; but as we have noted also, the religion of the state was a political affair.

It was on political grounds, therefore, that Christianity was opposed. True, from time to time other 'foreign gods' were 'banished', but between, say, Mithras or Isis and Christ there were enormous differences. First, no-one had ever seen Mithras or Isis – or Serapis or any of them. They had no corporal existence. Christ, on the other hand, had been seen by a very large number of people in one of the most populous regions of the Roman world.

For long the attitude of the state towards the Christians was curiously undefined. By the end of the first century, Christianity had won adherents not only in Rome but throughout the empire, and in every rank of society. The idea that the faith appealed only to the poor and lowly is mistaken. The majority of its adherents were poor, it is true, and that for two reasons. The first is that in a slave society based, as the Roman one was, on the exploitation of the poor by the rich, the poor were bound to be in the majority; and that a religion such as Christianity which made a universal appeal was bound to attract more of the humble than of the exalted. The second reason is to be found in the innate conservatism which, as has already appeared many times in this

brief study, characterised the Roman mind. Indeed, the very words *novas res*, new things, were an accepted synonym for sedition. Nevertheless from the very outset Christianity did attract men and women in the upper brackets of society. Joseph of Arimathea, Joanna the wife of Herod's steward, Sergius Paulus governor of Cyprus, Publius the chief citizen of Malta – these were but the first of many. Thus, while the faith grew and consolidated itself into an organised society – something which none of the pagan importations ever succeeded in achieving – it drew into its orbit not merely those lowly souls who longed for *salus*, salvation or spiritual health, but men and women of intellect as well.

The Christians knew exactly

whither they were bound, in this life and the next; the Roman state did not. That is why its policy in regard to Christianity wavered. The Roman church historian Eusebius, who lived in the fourth century, tells us that Ulpian, the great jurist of the preceding century, compiled a catalogue of all the imperial edicts relating to Christianity (to which Ulpian was hostile). This has not come down to us, having naturally been suppressed when the emperors were themselves Christian. We can only piece together therefore a rather ragged history of the struggle between church and state. Nero's onslaught has been mentioned; but that was a mere shift, not an act of policy. Domitian in the last years of the first century attacked Christians, but then Domitian attacked anyone

who refused to recognise him as lord and god. The first documentary evidence we have of the state's attitude to Christianity comes from the year 112. The emperor Trajan had sent as governor of Bithynia, a key province, a personal friend of his called Pliny, the famous nephew of an admiral and encyclopedist who had lost his life while trying to rescue friends during the eruption of Vesuvius which had destroyed Pompeii in A.D. 79. Pliny like his uncle was a man of letters rather than of action, and so he was always referring difficult problems to his master. Pliny reports that he had come in contact with people called Christians. What was he to do about them? They weren't really bad, he thought, but there was no denying that they 'assembled and met togeth-

er'. To us, that hardly seems a criminal act; but in a world where any form of association, even a trade guild, might be regarded as subversive, it was a serious charge. Indeed, on another occasion when Pliny wrote to Trajan saying that there had been a serious fire in one of his cities and that he proposed to allow the enrolment of a regular fire-brigade 'of carefully controlled numbers', Trajan refused to give his consent. He was convinced they would form a political cell and conspire against the state. So he writes to Pliny about the Christians: 'Nothing can be laid down as a general ruling, involving something like a set form of procedure. They are not to be sought out; but if they are accused and convicted they must be punished'. But no attention was to be paid to anonymous accusations which were 'unworthy of our age'.

Even Trajan, Rome's greatest soldier, the man who carried the empire to its widest bounds, even he could give no precise direction on this point. His successor, Hadrian, the universal genius as H. A. L. Fisher called him, continued this ambiguous policy as we know from a letter of his to the governor of Asia. The government never seemed to make up its mind about the new religion. Perhaps it would fade away, as so many cults had done before: perhaps like them it was really not so subversive after all. Many people who knew Christians found them not only warm-hearted folk but good citizens as well. But even in the first years of Christendom there were outbreaks against it which ended in martyrdoms. It was

Left and right. Julius Caesar (100–44 B.C.). This bust brings out Caesar's far-sighted and ruthless determination. He was deified after his death, thereby setting an imperial fashion which contributed so direly to the dispute between Rome and the Christians. British Museum, London.

Opposite left. Tiberius, emperor from A.D. 14 to 37, the Caesar of the Gospels, deliberately rebutted any attempt to regard him as divine.

Opposite right. Fortuna. Fortune, rather than Fors, (chance) was in fashion in classical Rome. She was identified with the Greek Tyche. She is represented with a horn of plenty, and a rudder, as in this statue from the port of Ostia, because it is Fortune who 'steers' men's lives. Her most important temple was at Praeneste Palestrina. It contained an oracle whose hierophant replied through mysterious letters known as the sortes praenestinae. Musei Vaticani.

generally the mob that started them, not the government, which only intervened to appease the populace by slaughtering the Christians. This may have been the fate of Ignatius who was sent to Rome and there executed in Trajan's time; it certainly was the fate of Polycarp and his companions who were martyred at Smyrna in or about the year 155. In 177 a throng of Christians was butchered amid scenes of revolting cruelty at Lyons. Except for such sporadic outbreaks the Christians remained tolerated, but no more: they asked again and again to have their status defined and recognised, but always without success. When proceedings were taken against them the aim of the magistrate, from the days of Pliny onwards, was to persuade rather than to punish: the government wanted apostasy not martyrdom.

What gave rise to this curiously vague attitude, this so un-Roman ambivalence, in regard to the Christians? What in the eyes of the law was their crime? No one charge covers every instance. Let us go back to Tacitus, our earliest pagan source. Tacitus had been governor of Asia at about the same time as his friend Pliny was administering Bithynia, so he must have been familiar with Christians

and their beliefs. He writes of their genesis as follows: 'Christus, from whom the name had its origin, suffered the extreme penalty at the hands of one of our procurators, Pontius Pilate; and a deadly superstition thus checked for the moment again broke out not only in Judaea, the source of the evil, but also in the city, where all things hideous and shameful from every part of the world meet and become popular.'

The founder of the new faith was a condemned criminal, executed for a political offence – that was the basic fact from which loyal citizens and good Romans should recoil. It followed that those who not merely venerated but actually worshipped a criminal must themselves be criminal. The Christians were aware of this, which is why in the first centuries, as already mentioned, they were chary of using the crucifix as a symbol. They preferred to represent Jesus as the sun-god (as in the now famous Vatican mosaic), or, very commonly, as the good shepherd, or as the child with his mother, often attended by the Magi.

The second point which the state had to take into account was the attitude of the Christians to the state. This was, in brief, that while they felt

themselves bound to pray for Caesar and to render unto him, as their Master had taught them, the things which were his, they were unable to pray to him.

The Divine Emperors

Here we must digress for a moment to enquire how it had become the fashion, indeed, the rule, for anyone to pray to Caesar.

The god-king was an ancient eastern institution. In Egypt the pharoah had for thousands of years been regarded as a god. When, after Alexander's conquest, a Greek dynasty replaced the pharoahs, it was only natural that they, too, should be worshipped as divine – indeed, Alexander himself, by making his celebrated pilgrimage to the shrine of Ammon, had acquired in the eyes of many of his subjects the aura of divinity. The Roman conception of divinity has already been discussed: it amounted originally to little more than a belief in survival. To declare a man divus was utterly different from the Christian belief that the one and only God had become Man. This lay at the root of the quarrel. To a Christian to call a man divine was blasphemy. Yet this is precisely what the Romans tended to do more and more. Julius Caesar had been deified after his death. Augustus, prudent as always, while calling himself *Divi filius* – the son of a deity – was careful not to claim divinity himself. It would have outraged Roman sentiment to have hailed a *living* Roman as divine. He nevertheless permitted the veneration of his *genius*. In fact despite his politic scruples he was hailed as divine, not only in the ardent east, but even in Rome itself. Virgil sang of the peace which Augustus had created that it was the work of 'some god' – *deus nobis haec otia fecit*. Horace, in a laureate ode has a picture of Augustus lying at ease between two pagan gods sipping his nectar with purple lips – *quos inter Augustus recumbens purpureo bibit ore nectar*, a phrase which shocked Victorian editors, who thought that Roman ideas of divinity were the same as their own. As we have seen, they were not: and it is just this very difference, it must once again be emphasised, that caused the centuries-long rift between Christian and pagan. They were simply not using the same words in the same sense. Roman ideas of deity, may it be once more repeated, were vague, undogmatic. Even Fortune, for instance, could be regarded as a goddess. She was the firstborn of Jupiter, she helped women in childbirth. Her cult-statue was *Fortuna Primigenia*, 'the First Mother'. At Praeneste, (Palestrina) she had a splendid temple, which housed an oracle. She was powerful, she was important, and yet how vague were Roman ideas about Fortune and her 'wheel'!

As with Fortune, so it was with the divinity of the Caesars. Augustus's successor Tiberius, always conscientiously following his predecessor's precepts, deliberately rebutted attempts to regard him as divine. 'I must confess I'm mortal' he said. Domitian claimed divinity, but the divinity of the emperors was by no means yet an accepted axiom. On the death of Claudius, Seneca wrote a skit called 'Pumpkinification' mocking the idea. Vespasian, the successor of Nero, joked about it: 'I think I'm becoming a god' he said as death approached. Nevertheless, what had

started as flattery gradually hardened into faith. The late Mrs Eugénie Strong, our leading authority on Roman sculpture, had argued most persuasively that the custom of representing an emperor as the central figure in a group on a temple, the very place formerly held by gods in Greek sculpture, helped to foster the idea that this central figure was in fact divine. Which is rather like transferring a statue from a transept of Westminster Abbey to a niche above the high altar. This is the process which the cult oi the emperor underwent. Caesar was god, and unto him alone must be rendered the things which belonged to both. No Christian could do it.

Reaction to Christianity

Slanders which arose from Christian modes of worship were the third factor in the State's reaction to Christianity. As we learn from *Acts*, the first Christians gathered for worship in private houses. This custom continued, and the earliest Christian churches in Rome, e.g. S. Martino ai Monti, S. Pudenziana or SS. Giovanni e Paolo, are actually built over the houses they superseded. In these houses baptised believers would meet before dawn to celebrate the Eucharist, which was both (as its name implies) a thanksgiving and a love-feast. People knew that to the participants an oath or *sacramentum* was administered, of which the outward and visible form was the consuming of 'the body and blood of the Son of Man'; also that the Christians addressed one another as brothers and sisters. In addition to accusations of conspiracy, malicious imputations of cannibalism and incest were soon in circulation.

Many respectable people believed them including one of the tutors of Marcus Aurelius.

These three sources of hostility combined to make the mere name of Christian an offence, because it was known that the Christians were extremely resolute. They could not and would not compromise. Their obstinacy was proverbial: Marcus Aurelius himself cites it. Finally there was the demeanour and behaviour of the Christians. Some pagans there were, and always would be, who regulated their lives by the principles of Zeno or Epicurus, who were as blameless as Virgil; but the general tone of society was lewd and brutal to a degree which it is hard for us, the heirs of so many Christian centuries, to comprehend. Society resented, as society always does, those who did not share its vices. It disliked the Christians on principle.

But the leaven was at work. More and more souls sought and found in the Christian faith that which they found nowhere else – support and solace. In the second century the Church was strong enough to start commending itself in literary form. The New Testament was the Christians' own guide; but they felt that a different approach was needed to reach not only the hearts but the minds of the unconverted. The first apologists appeared in the days of Hadrian (117-138). They wrote in Greek, which was not only the language of culture but even of the Roman church itself until the middle of the third century. The earliest apology which we possess is that of Aristides, an Athenian philosopher, who addressed it to Antoninus, Hadrian's successor. His purpose is simply to explain who the Christians are, who Jesus was, what he taught. Aristides' work is what we should call a religious tract. That was all it was meant to be. His contemporary Justin of Neapolis (Nablus) in Palestine is a man of a more formidable calibre. His search for truth had led him to many a shrine, until finally he was converted to Christianity, and settled in Rome, where he opened a school of instruction and died as a martyr in 165. Justin, three of whose works we still possess, is not content with proving merely that the Christians are not atheists: he sets out to demonstrate that their doctrine is founded in antiquity and is consonant with Greek philosophy. He explains the doctrine of the *Logos*, or Word, which was familiar to both Greek and Jewish philosophers and forms the grand exordium to the Gospel of St John.

Justin was followed by others who like himself came from the eastern provinces. During the last two decades of the century Alexandria possessed a spiritual beacon, a true Pharos of the soul, in Clement. To give some idea of his insight and outlook one quotation must suffice. It is of great importance because it was just this veneration of conservatism which he assails which was to be sharpened into persecution in the following century. Clement is all for progress; but the Christians were not revolutionaries. Here is Clement's

answer to the accusation, from his *Protrepticus*, or Hortative (X, 89):

'You say it is unreasonable to overthrow a way of life that has been handed down from our forefathers. In that case why do we not go on using our first food, milk, to which as you will admit, our nurses accustomed us from birth? Why do we add to or diminish our family property, instead of keeping it at the same value as when we received it? . . . So in life itself, shall we not abandon the old way, which is wicked, full of passion and without God? And shall we not, even at the risk of displeasing our fathers, set our course towards the truth and look for him who is our real father, discarding custom like some deadly drug? There is no doubt that the noblest of all the tasks we have in hand is simply this: to prove to you that it was from madness, and from this thrice miserable *custom* that hatred of godliness sprang. . . . Let us shake off the ignorance and darkness that spreads like a mist over our sight; and let us get a vision of the true God,

first raising to him this voice of praise: "Hail O Light". Upon us who lay buried in darkness and shut up in the "shadow of death" a "light shone forth" from heaven, purer than the sun and sweeter than the life of earth. That light is life eternal, and whatsoever things share in it, live. But night shrinks back from the light, and setting through fear, gives place to the day of the Lord. . . . He it was who changed the setting into a rising, changed crucified death into life. He snatched man out of the jaws of destruction. He raised him into the sky, transplanting corruption to the soil of incorruption, and transforming earth to heaven.'

Here indeed was a new clarion, a trumpet challenge to conformity. No pagan had written with such jubilant confidence for many a long, bleak, year.

Clement was followed by others as eloquent. One of the most famous was a fiery Carthaginian called Tertullian, who was born in the former Punic capital about the year 160.

Here is an excerpt from his famous *Apology*, in which he refutes the charge of the Christians' disloyalty:

'We on behalf of the emperors invoke the eternal God, the true God, the living God, whom the emperors prefer to have propitious to them beyond all other gods. They know who has given them the empire, they know as men who has given them life; they feel that he is God alone, in whose power and no other's they are, second to whom they stand, after whom they come first, before all gods and above all gods. . . . Looking up to heaven the Christians – with hands outspread because innocent, with head bare because we do not blush, yes and without anyone to dictate the form of words because we pray from the heart – we are continually making intercession for the emperors. We beseech for them a long life, a secure rule, a safe home, brave armies, a faithful senate, an honest people, a quiet world – and everything for which a man and a Caesar can pray.'

Could loyalty be more beautifully

consecrated? Other eloquent and persuasive apologists were to appear before the end of the century, of whom the greatest was Origen, who was born in Egypt of Christian parents about 185. He towers above his age, both as scholar and propagandist. He was received at the imperial court. It even looked as though Christianity was about to be recognised as a 'permitted religion'. But nothing is so illogical as history: far from being allowed to live in peace, the Christian faith was about to undergo its greatest trial, nothing less than an attempt to stamp it out altogether.

Persecution and Triumph

The Church was now a highly efficient polity, vocal, vigorous and literate. The state might well wonder whether it would be wise to abolish it or to come to terms with it. In the event the state tried both solutions. During the third century, Rome sank into decay and disorder – what one of Rome's historians described as the age of iron and rust following the gold of the age of the Antonines. Anarchy within was aggravated by invasion from without, the first waves of the barbarian flood which was to engulf the Roman world in the fifth

Above left. Claudius, emperor from A.D. 41 to 54 owed his elevation largely to his Jewish friend Agrippa of Judaea. When he was 'deified' Seneca wrote a biting satire on the topic. Musei Vaticani.

Above right. Nero, emperor A.D. 54–68, last of the Julio-Claudians, and the first persecutor of the Christians.

Opposite. Marcus Aurelius, the philosopher emperor (A.D. 161–180) is here shown sacrificing, his head veiled in accordance with Roman custom. The temple in the background gives an excellent impression of what a Roman temple looked like in its pristine splendour. Museo Capitolino, Rome.

Opposite. A Christian catacomb. Catacombs were places of burial. The corpses were generally left in the niches until they had decomposed, when the bones would be removed to a central repository, to make way for new tenants. Catacombs were not, and could not be 'secret meeting-places'. The first Christians met in houses, which were often later transformed into churches. Rome still has several examples of these house-churches.

Above. This mosaic of the third century A.D. from Casale (Piazza Armerina) in Sicily is an excellent example of the Roman love of *narrative* art. It shows a hunting party, just returned from the chase, sacrificing to Diana, the chase's patroness.

Right. Vespasian, who with his son Titus, subdued Judaea. Emperor from A.D.69 to 79. 'I think I'm becoming a god', he said sarcastically as death approached. Museo Archeologico Nazionale, Naples.

century. The psychological reaction to these pitiful events was exactly what Clement would have foreseen: a return to *custom*, the old beliefs, the old formulae, the old altars. It was the Christians, men said, who were responsible for the woes of Rome. They must be done away with. Thus broke out the last, organised persecutions. It was Decius (249-251) who started them, and they continued sporadically for the rest of the century and on into the next.

But during these years of decay a religious revival took place which was by one of the ironies of fate to pave the way for the triumph of Christianity. Monotheism had become to all intents and purposes the religion of the state. Not the monotheism of the Jews and Christians, but a solar monotheism. '*Sol invictus*', the unconquered sun, became more and more the ruling deity of the Roman pantheon. Augustus had recognised the sun as a deity. He had brought from Egypt two obelisks, and had erected them in Rome as 'gifts to the sun' (not yet 'the unconquered sun'). Both these obelisks, together with the inscriptions, still stand in the city.

A succession of emperors had actively patronised and promoted the cult. In the year 305 Constantius became one of the two *Augusti*, between whom, with their two subordinate *Caesars*, the government of the empire was now divided as the result of Diocletian's reforms. By his wife, Helena, Constantius had a son called Constantine. His father died at York in 306, and the troops hailed Constantine as emperor. He was a remarkable man, of a truly spiritual cast. He had been brought up as a worshipper of the 'unconquered sun'; but as the result of what he deemed to be a divine revelation he was converted to the Christian faith. In 313 the so-called 'Edict of Milan' freed the Christian religion, which thereafter became the established religion of the empire.

But paganism lived on. The pontifical college still met, the Vestal virgins watched over their undying fire, the feast of the Great Mother was still celebrated. The statue of Victory which Augustus had placed in the Senate-house, evicted by Constantine's successor, restored by Julian, again evicted and again restored, was only finally dislodged at the insistence of St Ambrose in 391. Roman society was still led by cultivated pagans – or orthodox conservatives as they regarded themselves. Only in the year 392 did the emperor Theodosius issue the edict which put an end to paganism, that is to toleration and religious freedom.

In our own day, both have been restored. We can contemplate the whole long pilgrimage which had led mankind from the Tiber to the Lake of Geneva, thence to the Thames, and now back to the Tiber. Caesar made a pact with Christ: Caesar is forgotten, so, by many, is Christ, but so long as men turn to the spirit when the body falters and fails, it is to Rome with all its history, all its mythology, all its reality that they will be drawn.

Further Reading List

Altheim, F. (Tr. H. Mattingley) *A History of Roman Relgion* (2 vols). Methuen, 1938.

Ashby, T. *Some Italian Scenes and Festivals.* Methuen, 1929.

Bailey, C., *Phases in the Religion of Ancient Rome,* Oxford University Press, 1932.

Bloch, Raymond. *The Origins of Rome.* Thames and Hudson, 1960.

Cambridge Ancient History, vol. viii, ch. xix vol. x, ch. xv vol. xii, chs. xii, xiii, xiv, xv, xix. Cambridge University Press.

Cary, M., etc. (Ed.), *The Oxford Classical Dictionary.* Oxford 1949.

Cumont, F., *After Life in Roman Paganism.* Dover Publications Inc., New York, 1959. *Oriental Religions in Roman Paganism.* Dover Publications Inc., New York, 1956.

Fowler, W. Warde, *The Religious Experience of the Roman People.* Macmillan, 1940. *Roman Ideas of Deity.* Macmillan, 1914.

Frazer, Sir J. G., *The Fasti of Ovid.* Heinemann, 1929.

Grant, Frederick C., *Ancient Roman Religion.* Liberal Arts Press, 1957.

Grant, M., *Myths of the Greeks and Romans.* Weidenfeld & Nicolson, 1962; Mentor Books, New English Library, 1965. *The Roman World.* Weidenfeld and Nicolson, 1960.

Grimal, Pierre. *Dictionnaire de la Mythologie Grecque et Romaine.* Pressey Universitaires de France, 1958.

Halliday, W. R. *Greek and Roman Folklore.* Harrap, 1927.

Harris, Eve and John. *The Oriental Cults in Roman Britain.* Brill (Leiden), 1965.

Perowne, S. *Caesars and Saints.* Hodder & Stoughton, 1962. *The End of the Roman World.* Hodder & Stoughton, 1966.

Rose, H. J. *Ancient Roman Religion.* Hutchinson, 1949.

Rostovtzeff. M. *Rome.* Oxford University Press, 1960.

Smith, W. (Ed.), *A Dictionary of Greek and Roman Biography and Mythology* (3 vols). London, 1876.

Strong, Mrs Arthur. *Apotheosis and After Life.* Constable, 1915.

Taylor, L. R. *The Divinity of the Roman Emperors.* Middletown, 1932. (Philological monographs pub. by American Philosophical Association, No. 1).

Warner, Rex. *Men and Gods.* Penguin Books, Harmondsworth, 1952.

And relevant articles in

Hastings' Encyclopedia of Religion and Ethics. T. & T. Clark, 1908.

The Jewish Encyclopedia. Funk and Wagnalls, New York, 1901.

New Catholic Encyclopedia. McGraw Hill Book Company, New York and London, 1967.

Acknowledgments

Photographs. Alinari, Florence 16, right 19 right, 33 bottom, 52 left, 52 right, 54 bottom left, 60 right, 61 bottom, 84-85, 112 top right, 112 centre right, 112 bottom right; Anderson, Florence 14 bottom, 25, 41, 70-71, 89 left, 89 right, 95, 116 top, 141; Archiv für Kunst und Geschichte, Berlin 96-97; J. E. Bulloz, Paris 48; British Museum, London, 36; Deutsches Archaeologisches Institut, Rome 32-33; C. M. Dixon, Dover 6-7, 107, 111; Fotoceca Unione, Rome 15 top, 28, 43 top, 54 bottom right, 124, 140; Gabinetto Fotografico Nazionale, Rome 99; Photographie Giraudon, Paris 18, 29 right, 40 left, 40 right, 40-41, 79; Sonia Halliday Photographs, Weston Turville 67 top, 139 top; Hamlyn Group Picture Library 14 bottom right, 34, 50, 57 right, 82-83, 105 bottom left, 105 bottom right, 106, 114 top; M. Holford, Loughton 10 top, 10 bottom, 31; Librairie Hachette, Paris 120, Mansell Collection, London 9, 13 left, 13 right, 14 top left, 14 top right, 16 left, 17, 19 bottom left, 20, 21, 26-27, 29 left, 37, 39, 41 left, 41 centre, 44 top, 44 bottom, 45 top, 45 centre, 45 bottom, 46 top, 53, 56, 57 left, 60 left 60 centre, 60-61, 61 top, 64 top, 64 bottom left, 64 bottom right, 65, 68, 69 left, 70, 71, 77, 81, 93, 101, 108-109, 112 left, 117, 121, 125, 126-127, 129, 132 left, 132 right, 133 right, 135, 136 right, 137; Mansell – Alinari 16-17, 92, 109, 113, 116 bottom; Mansell – Anderson 68-69, 114 bottom 138, 139 bottom; Editrice Bemporad Marzocco, Florence 119; Musée du Bardo, Algiers 80; Musei Vaticani 136 left; Museo della Civiltà Romana, Rome 33 top, 33 centre, 44 bottom; Museum of London 91; Photoresources, Dover 15 bottom, 42 top, 42 bottom, 67 bottom, 87, 90, 94, 102, 118, 131, 134; Pictorial Press, London 133 left; Paul Popper, London 69 right; Roger-Viollet, Paris 104 bottom; Scala, Antella 11, 22, 23, 38, 50-51, 54 top, 55, 58-59, 62, 66, 82, 115; R. V. Schoder, Chicago, Illinois 63, 75, 122-123, 123; Soprintendenza alle Antichità di Roma (Scavi di Ostia), Rome 46 bottom; M. Stapleton, London 47; Michele Vellente, Loreto Aprutino 26; Warburg Institute, London 105 top; Ziolo – André Held 2, 83, 86, 130.

Index